D1523186

In Exile:
The History and Lore Surrounding New Orleans Gay Culture and Its Oldest Gay Bar

Frank Perez
and
Jeffrey Palmquist

In Exile:
The History and Lore
Surrounding New Orleans Gay Culture and Its Oldest Gay Bar

ISBN: 9781905091997
Paperback Version
© 2012 by Frank Perez and Jeffrey Palmquist

Published in the United Kingdom by LL-Publications 2012
www.ll-publications.com
57 Blair Avenue
Hurlford
Scotland
KA1 5AZ

Edited by Zetta Brown
Proofreading by Billye Johnson
Book layout and typesetting by jimandzetta.com
Cover art and design by Helen E. H. Madden www.pixelarcana.com © 2011
Additional photographs appear with permission at the courtesy of Jeffrey
Palmquist, The Historic New Orleans Collection, SouthernDecadence.com,
and Wood Enterprises

Printed in the UK, USA, and Australia

In Exile: The History and Lore Surrounding New Orleans Gay Culture and its Oldest Gay Bar is
a work of nonfiction. The names of a few select people have been changed to protect
anonymity.

All rights reserved. No part of this publication may be copied, transmitted, or
recorded by any means whatsoever, including printing, photocopying, file transfer, or
any form of data storage, mechanical or electronic, without the express written
consent of the publisher. In addition, no part of this publication may be lent, re-sold,
hired, or otherwise circulated or distributed, in any form whatsoever, without the
express written consent of the publisher.

Praise for IN EXILE

"A true look into New Orleans Gay History and Café Lafitte's role in it."

—Ken GranPré, General Manger Wood Enterprises, Café Lafitte

"Even further back than the oldest gay publication in the South, an exciting read..."

—*Ambush* Magazine

"A perfect reflection of the French Quarter, *In Exile* brings history to piquant, steamy, and always-fascinating life. The Quarter is a place like no other, and with the publication of *In Exile*, there's now a book about its history like no other."

—Rick R. Reed, award-winning author of *Caregiver*

Dedication

For Josh and Tracey

Acknowledgments

MANY PEOPLE CONTRIBUTED TO THIS PROJECT. Because no comprehensive history of gay New Orleans exists and because primary source material is scarce, we have relied heavily on the recollections of scores of men who agreed to be interviewed. To them, we are grateful. Just as many people who preferred not to be formally interviewed offered encouragement throughout the research and writing process. Still others were willing to share their own research with us, notably Gilbert Estrada, whose scrapbooks of newspaper articles concerning the gay community were a treasure trove of research. Otis Fennel, owner of the Faubourg Marigny Arts and Books, graciously apprised us of previous research efforts and suggested several fruitful interview subjects. Ken GranPré, general manager of Wood Enterprises, provided early photographs of Lafitte's and offered invaluable suggestions of people to be interviewed. Leon Cahill Miller and Ann E. Smith Case of the Louisiana Research Collection at the Howard-Tilton Memorial Library were extremely helpful in helping us navigate the extensive archives of GLBT ephemera at Tulane University. Dr. John Meyers' enthusiasm and encouragement were invaluable and much appreciated. We are also grateful to untold thousands of gay men over the decades who, by living their lives openly and with dignity, nudged the closet door ever more open. Their names have slipped from memory and their lives remain unsung. Their legacy does not.

Pedestrian on Canal Street: *"Where is the Canal Street Ferry?"*

Tinkerbell, beloved Lucky Dog Vendor: *"Here I am, Darling."*

*   *   *

"Apparently the French Quarter of New Orleans has an atmosphere which appeals to these people, who are an undesirable element in our community."

—Colonel Provosty A. Dayries, New Orleans Superintendent of Police
(Excerpt from a letter dated July 24, 1958 written to other police departments seeking advice on how to handle the problem of homosexuals and lesbians.)

*   *   *

"There is no such thing as a gay sensibility and it has had an enormous impact on the culture."

—Jeff Weinstein

*   *   *

"Homosexual relationships can be, and frequently are happy. Men live together for years and make homes and share their lives and their work, just as heterosexuals do . . . Certainly, under the present social set up, a homosexual relationship is more difficult to maintain than a heterosexual one, but doesn't that merely make it more of a challenge and therefore, in a sense, more humanly worthwhile? The success of such a relationship is revolutionary in the best sense of the word. And, because it demonstrates the power of human affection over fear and prejudice and taboo, it is actually beneficial to society as a whole—as all demonstrations of faith and courage must be: they raise our collective morale."

—Christopher Isherwood, 1948
(Quoted in Charles Kaiser's *The Gay Metropolis*)

Table of Contents

Part Four
The 1980s: The Closet Door Falls Off Its Hinges

A Little Decadence Goes a Long Way
Midgets, Poppers, and a Whole Lot of DNA
The Plague
Bartenders, Drug Addicts, and Other Characters
Ambush

Part Five
The 1990s & 2000s: Yellow Brick Roads Emerge from the Closet

On Balconies
Legal Strides in the 1990s
An Afternoon at the Faerie Playhouse
Gay Life Outside the Bars
Radical Faeries
King Cake Queens
One Does Want a Hint of Leather
Santa Claus is Gay
Katrina: The Gay Community Blows Back
Yellow Brick Roads
Our Personal Journeys

Part Six
Epilogue

A Good Mix
The View from Behind the Bar
A Mutual Affinity
The Granddaddy of Them All

Appendices

Appendix A: Gay Bars Throughout New Orleans History
Appendix B: Historical Timeline of Gay Mardi Gras
Appendix C: Southern Decadence Grand Marshals
Appendix D: Victims of The Upstairs Lounge Fire
Appendix E: Early Gay Activists in New Orleans
Appendix F: Prominent Gay New Orleanians

Bibliography and Index

Introduction

IT IS EARLY SATURDAY MORNING. As day gradually usurps night, I sit pensively in Jackson Square. The cobblestone banquettes are shiny with wet for the street cleaners have just made their rounds washing away the remains of yesterday. Nearby a few homeless people sleep on benches sitting upright while a pigeon or two search in vain for crumbs. For the most part, the Square is empty, save a few faithful awaiting early morning mass. A family of tourists ambles by with their luggage. In the corner, a fortune teller shuffles her tarot cards. An old man walks his dog. The stench of trash fills the air as a garbage truck shares the streets with several produce delivery trucks bringing what will be, in a few hours, brunch. A strong breeze from the river is blowing.

The Cathedral bells ring and about two-dozen people file into the church for Mass, me included. No, I am not here to worship nor am I here to eat *ecce pannis angelorum*; I am here to *imagine*. You see, for me, St. Louis Cathedral (and the French Quarter in general) is a time machine. As the liturgy drones on, I imagine what it must have been like 200 years ago when this church would have been packed for an early morning Lenten Mass. This ability to awaken a sense of history—to really make the past come alive—is one of the qualities that make the French Quarter so magical.

After the Mass has ended, I sit in the Square chatting with an ancient nun, dressed in full pre-Vatican II regalia. She is disappointed to learn I will not be attending Mass regularly but informs me I am welcome anytime. Her wrinkled face offers me a smile and a blessing and she departs for whatever her day has for her, part of which will no doubt include cyclical recitations of the Rosary. As she wanders off down St. Ann, I wonder what she will think of the men sitting in the gay bars a few blocks away she will pass momentarily. Perhaps she will give them no thought at all. Nor they her. Not far away, the oldest gay bar in the country peacefully coexists a few blocks away from the oldest Roman Catholic convent in the country. That's about as New Orleans as it gets.

Many words come to mind when one thinks of "New Orleans" but my favorite is *mélange*, a word that comes to us from the seventeenth century French word *mêler*, which means "to mix and mingle" and which has its etymological roots in the Old French word *mesler*, which in the Renaissance was a euphemism for sexual intercourse. Yes, *mélange* is the perfect word to describe New Orleans for what else is this city but a multicultural orgy producing a linguistic, ethnic, culinary, musical, and architectural fusion—disparate histories and cultural traditions melding, blending, coalescing, uniting, yet each one never quite losing its own identity. Ezra Pound might call it the urban embodiment of vorticism.

These thoughts are heavy, too heavy to bear without coffee so I walk a block to Café du Monde. Abandoning medieval French etymology, my mind turns to chicory. Chicory is a staple ingredient in virtually all New Orleans coffee. A derivative of the endive plant, chicory has been a coffee additive (and sometimes a substitute) for centuries. The chicory flower is thought to be the inspiration of the *Blaue Blume*, a central symbol in German Romanticism that represents desire and metaphysical yearning for the unattainable and the infinite—two universal concepts at the heart of Romanticism and essential to any brand of hedonism. No wonder New Orleanians love chicory!

The chicory's stimulating quality casts a spell on me and I consider the *Blaue Blume* in terms of the mystery of sexual identity. What makes the intersection of sexuality and the urban space we call New Orleans so unique, so electric, so free?

Something about New Orleans renders difference irrelevant, makes it melt. Melt is a good word to describe the Quarter. Everything seems to melt here: cares, worries, inhibitions. Especially inhibitions. A prominent eighteenth century nun observed in a letter to her family back in France, "The Devil here possesses a large empire"[1] (Dawdy 2). But not just morality, other things melt too: cultures, ethnicities, architecture, cuisine, music, languages. And sexualities. It's not so much evanescence but rather mutability, a melting into each other, like the outlying marsh and swamp where land melts into sea. History melts too, if we let it.

Four hours after his first arrival in New Orleans, Tennessee Williams wrote in his journal, "Here, surely, is the place I was made for." It is likely that his first sexual experience with a man occurred a few nights later. Williams would later call New Orleans his "spiritual home" and the French Quarter "the last frontier of Bohemia." As he once wrote to a friend, "Town is *wide* open."[2]

Wide open indeed. Never burdened by the Puritanical baggage that straddles so many other American cities, New Orleans has always enjoyed a certain permissiveness. Hedonism permeates the air, so to speak. The city's history and reputation for letting the good times roll is well documented: Storyville and its hookers, jazz-filled bordellos, opium dens, the birth of the cocktail, the introduction of Craps to the New World, Carnival, the non-stop drinking, etc. But a significant part of New Orleans' debauched past remains curiously hidden.

Despite the progress made in recent years, much of American gay history remains in the closet. This is certainly true of New Orleans. And that's a shame. After all, New Orleans, throughout its colorful and picaresque history, has inspired and offered refuge to multitudes of gay writers, artists, musicians, and philanthropists. At some point during their time in New Orleans, each one of them, along with thousands of anonymous others undoubtedly darkened the door of

---

[1] The nun was Marie-Madeleine Hachard.

[2] The quotes in this paragraph are taken from Roberts Batson's entry on New Orleans in the on-line gay encyclopedia glbtq.com. Batson is considered the premiere historian on gay New Orleans and his entry on New Orleans in the glbtq encyclopedia was invaluable during the initial research stages of this book.

In Exile

America's oldest gay bar—Café Lafitte in Exile.

In Exile: The History and Lore Surrounding New Orleans Gay Culture and Its Oldest Gay Bar is an effort to shed light on gay New Orleans hidden past. Much of that history was written by firelight in a small bar on the quiet end of Bourbon Street. Known to regulars simply as "Lafitte's," this bar served as the epicenter of gay life in New Orleans for decades. And it's still going strong. Drawn primarily on the recollections of those who patronized the bar over the last fifty years, here are the stories of countless gay lives: bartenders and hustlers, drag queens and closet cases, literary giants and movie stars, people like you and me. Read and then close your eyes and re-live their tales of youthful discovery, fear of disclosure, naïve hopes, lustful desires, sexual ecstasy, subsequent addictions, broken dreams, incredible loss, and, for the lucky ones, ultimate redemption.

In the process, succumb to New Orleans' inevitable charm. Join the multitude of scores who have made William Faulkner's description of New Orleans ring fabulously true:

> A courtesan, not old and no longer young, who shuns the sunlight that the illusion of her former glory be preserved. The mirrors in her house are dim and the frames are tarnished; all her house is dim and beautiful with age . . . those whom she receives. . . come to her through an eternal twilight . . . New Orleans . . . a courtesan whose hold is strong upon the mature, to whose charm the young must respond. And all who leave her. . . return to her when she smiles across her languid fan . . . New Orleans. (14)

Faulkner's description could easily be applied to Café Lafitte in Exile.

ANCIENT MYTHOLOGY is perhaps the greatest triumph of humankind's ability to imagine, and the Muses in particular

Introduction

are the personification of our greatest artistic and intellectual aspirations. Born of a coupling between Zeus and Mnemosyne (memory), their lineage suggests a timeless truth: that history and imagination are inextricably linked together. New Orleans, a city that embraces and respects its history, cannot help then but be a wellspring of creativity. Imagination provides meaning and understanding to knowledge; it helps us perceive and thus shape our various realities.

Much of gay history is lost and that is certainly regrettable. In the course of researching this book, we have asked gay New Orleanians—young and old—to remember. Their recollections form the core of the narrative that follows. And hopefully, this narrative will serve as a reference point from which the gay community in New Orleans can shape its future reality.

As much as this book is about the history of gay New Orleans and the gay histories of gay New Orleanians, it is also a book about New Orleans herself. It is part reporting, part revealing, part investigating, part questioning. It is partly scholarly, partly gossipy. It is wholly a love letter, not only to the city but also to the gay men and women who contribute greatly to her complexity and beauty. It is certainly not the last word on gay New Orleans; in fact, it barely scratches the surface. A thoroughly exhaustive, comprehensive history of gay New Orleans remains to be written; the present work is but a step in that direction. Here we have focused on the city's oldest gay bar, positioning that discussion in the larger context of gay New Orleans history. In the process, we have created a general timeline of the major events, people, and attitudes that have shaped the gay community in New Orleans over the last seventy-five years. It is our desire that this book will spur further research on the subject. To that end we have included several appendices that may prove useful to future researchers.

Frank Perez
New Orleans, 2011

Part One
Pre-1960: The Closet Door Creaks

RAINBOWS ARE ESSENTIALLY LIGHT AND IN THE BEGINNING THERE WAS DARKNESS. Gay culture in New Orleans was born in the 1950s; prior to that it went through a long gestation period dating back to the nineteenth century. To follow through with this metaphor, we can point to the founding of Café Lafitte in Exile in 1933 as its conception. In this section we look back and explore the historical and cultural milieu in which gay New Orleans culture was conceived and born. More specifically, we examine the social forces that gave rise to, and then suppressed, its growth.

Part One - Pre 1960: The Closet Door Creaks

Gay New Orleans Before the Bars

LONG BEFORE LASALLE CLAIMED LOUISIANA FOR FRANCE and 150 years before Bienville founded New Orleans, there was something queer about the Native American trading post on the sharp bend in the Mississippi River where the French Quarter now exists. Sixteenth century French and Spanish explorers were shocked to discover gender-bending Native Americans as they sailed upriver from the Gulf of Mexico. *Berdaches* (two-spirits) were men who adopted feminine mannerisms and performed work traditionally reserved for women. Even more shocking to the European explorers was the fact these *berdaches* were highly regarded by their tribes. In 1751, Jean Bernard Bossu wrote of the Choctaw Tribe, "They are morally quite perverted, and most of them are addicted to sodomy" (Bossu 169). Apparently the Great Spirit on this side of the Atlantic didn't have a problem with gayness.

The Church, of course, did have a problem with it, and with Christianity's conquest of the New World, indigenous gayness was forced into the closet. The first Louisiana Criminal Code prescribed a mandatory life sentence for indulging in "the abominable and detestable crime against nature" (Batson). Later, the penalty was reduced to ten years in prison; and, later still, to five years. The state's anti-sodomy law wasn't struck down by the courts until 2003[3]. Despite these social and legal obstacles, gay men and women lived in New Orleans from its inception unable to openly express their true natures yet making incredible contributions to the city's cultural growth nonetheless.

Some contemporary scholars theorize prominent businessman and early New Orleans philanthropist John McDonogh (1779-1850) was probably gay. A life-long bachelor

---

[3] Louisiana's sodomy law was struck down by the U.S. Supreme Court on June 26, 2003, as a result of the Court's decision in Lawrence v. Texas, No. 02-102 (U.S. June 26, 2003). The Louisiana sodomy law applied to both heterosexual and same-sex partners and was punishable with up to five years in prison/$2,000 fine. La. R.S. 14:89 (2002).

who was described as eccentric and reclusive, McDonogh amassed a fortune in the shipping business, the bulk of which he willed to New Orleans and his native Baltimore upon his death for the purpose of establishing schools for poor white and free black children. Many schools in New Orleans today still bear his name. McDonogh also donated much of the land which became City Park.

Perhaps the most famous gay man to live in New Orleans was Walt Whitman, (1819-1892) who arrived in the city in 1848. Whitman scholar Ed Folsom argues Whitman found his first person poetic voice in New Orleans and Nordette Adams of *The New Orleans Literature Examiner* writes, "The Crescent City directly influenced Whitman's beliefs about human rights and the power of the individual voice."

Scholar Robert K. Martin has noted that Whitman's New Orleans experience "had an important impact on his conception of male love" (1) as reflected in his homoerotic poems. In "Once I Pass'd Through a Populous City," a poem about New Orleans, he wrote, "I remember only a woman I casually met there who detain'd me for love of me." But Martin insightfully observes that this line was changed. Whitman's original line read: "I remember only the man who wandered with me, there, for love of me." In another poem, "I Saw in Louisiana a Live-Oak Growing," he exulted that the "rude, unbending, lusty" tree made him "think of manly love."[4]

Where Whitman met his trick, and how, is uncertain. Gay social networking for the purpose of finding sex partners has been around for centuries. Fifteenth century Florence, for example, had quite an extensive network, a Renaissance version of Craigslist or Grindr, if you will. It's safe to assume nineteenth century New Orleans also had such a network. We do know there was a "gay scene" at the time for it is referenced by Baron Ludwig Von Reizenstein, a German expatriate living in New Orleans in the 1850s who wrote a serial entitled *The Mysteries of New Orleans* for a subversive bohemian

---

[4] The quotes in this paragraph are taken from Robert K. Martin's entry Walt Whitman in the on-line encyclopedia glbtq.com.

newspaper.[5] Whatever gay-friendly bars existed in mid-nineteenth century New Orleans, if any, are lost to history. The earliest gay business establishment in New Orleans that we know of was a brothel run by a burly male madam known as Miss Big Nelly in the late 1800s. Reportedly, the house was the scene of "large scale, noisy interracial functions" (Batson). At the turn of the century, there was also The Frenchman's, a small jazz club in Storyville which was popular among cross-dressers (Brothers 201).

One of most talented gay men in New Orleans in the early twentieth century was Tony Jackson (1876-1921). Jackson was highly influential in the early development of jazz and was widely considered the unrivaled king of jazz pianists. Jackson's hit song "Pretty Baby" was written about another man. Composed in The Frenchman's saloon in the early years of the twentieth century, it was not published until 1916, and then with new lyrics tailored for Fanny Brice to perform in the Broadway musical *Passing Show*. After his death at age forty-four, he was remembered as "an epileptic, alcoholic, homosexual Negro genius" (Batson).

And were it not for Lyle Saxon (1891-1946), there may have never been any gay bars in the French Quarter; indeed, there may not have even been a French Quarter—surely not as we know it today. When Saxon arrived in 1919, the French Quarter was run down and essentially a slum. Saxon, a successful writer, promoted the Quarter as an artistic haven. Not only did he lead its architectural preservation, he was also instrumental in attracting writers and artists to the deteriorating neighborhood. In his biography of Saxon, James Thomas writes, "Gradually, Tallant concludes, the French Quarter—primarily because of Saxon's influence—became 'more an art

---

5 Baron Ludwig Von Reizenstein fled his native Germany at his father's urging because of a number of legal scandals. He arrived in New Orleans around 1850 where he began editing and writing for a number of German-language newspapers. *The Mysteries of New Orleans* was serialized from 1854 to 1855 in *Louisiana Staatz-Zeitung*. The entire work was translated into English by Steven Rowan in 2004.

colony, less an underworld'" (31). In fact, an easy argument can be made that Saxon single-handedly saved the Quarter from sure ruin and ultimate destruction. Saxon's final work, *The Friends of Joe Gilmore* (1948), is, in the words of gay historian Roberts Batson, "an affectionate tribute to his longtime valet and, possibly, lover."[6]

McDonogh, Whitman, Jackson, and Saxon's lives demonstrate the incredible contributions gay men were making to New Orleans in the decades before gay bars existed. They were here. They were queer. But they had no place to drink—at least not a place where they could truly be themselves. That would change in 1933.

Prohibition in New Orleans? Not So Much

JANUARY 16, 1920 WAS A DARK DAY FOR BARS IN AMERICA. That was the day America outlawed alcohol. For thirteen years, serving or drinking alcohol meant violating the U.S. Constitution. For the most part, New Orleans simply ignored Prohibition. Local authorities turned a blind eye as wine, liquor, and beer flowed freely in bars and restaurants throughout the city. Of course, some bars disappeared never to resurface. But many bars remained in operation even if barely underground. The Old Absinthe House didn't even bother to go underground. Speakeasies were ubiquitous, homemade hooch was all the rage and New Orleans remained, by far, the wettest city in the country during the reign of the Volstead Act.

Federal authorities were not amused. In 2008 *The Times-Picayune,* a newspaper that traditionally has been and remains ultra-conservative, published an article commemorating the 75th anniversary of the end of Prohibition. Journalist Todd A. Price noted:

> In 1923, federal authorities sent their best

---

[6] The quotes in this paragraph are taken from Roberts Batson's entry on New Orleans in the on-line gay encyclopedia glbtq.com.

undercover agent here to dry up the oceans of illegal alcohol still flowing. Isidor Einstein, a self-promoting "master of disguise" known nationwide as Izzy, arrived in New Orleans looking for booze. He found it moments later, when a cab driver offered to sell him a pint.

For the next 10 days, Izzy put together a list of more than 800 people violating the Volstead Act, the federal law that spelled out how Prohibition was enforced. Agents spent a week raiding speakeasies and arresting bootleggers. *The Times-Picayune* noted that when this offensive ended and the weekend arrived, liquor "flowed freely," seats at "thronged" cabarets were nearly impossible to find and "a number of old-timers declared New Orleans nightlife Saturday rivaled that of pre-Volsteadian days."[7]

At best, the Feds were a nuisance to New Orleans, a city that has never fully trusted "The Americans" to begin with. According to legend, when Louisiana was transferred from France to the United States in 1803, the American flag got stuck as it was being hoisted up the pole in Jackson Square. This was prophetic for the Americans were never truly successful in Americanizing the city. Well into the twentieth century, the city was divided into Creole and American sections, Canal Street being the dividing line. Even today New Orleans remains the most un-American city in America, a distinction often noted by visitors.

The native New Orleanians then were surprisingly ambivalent about their new status as Americans. By 1803, New Orleans had been founded by the French, acquired by the Spanish, turned over to France again, and infused with immigrants from all over Europe. Throw in involuntary immigration from Africa and you have a societal mentality that

---

[7] Price, Todd A. "New Orleans Bars Celebrate the 75th Anniversary of Prohibition's Repeal." *Times-Picayune* 5 Dec. 2008

never bought into, and still to this day resists, Anglo-Saxon Protestantism with all its oppressive morality and mistrust of monarchy and laborious work ethic and bland food. The late great A.J. Liebling had it right when he observed that "New Orleans is within the orbit of a Hellenistic world that never touched the North Atlantic" (87). And it's true. Even now it's easy to distinguish between visitors from Europe and say, Missouri or Ohio. Visitors from Spain or Italy or Greece look completely at ease; visitors from America's heartland look like freshmen on the first day of fall classes.

New Orleans has always been a drinking town. Alcohol was a leading import for most of the colonial period. Home brewing was popular too; in 1802, 100,140 empty bottles were imported to the city. New Orleans' first city tax was a tax on billiard tables and taverns. That was a profitable move; the 1791 census indicates half of all the merchants in the city were tavern keepers.

Long before the French arrived with their penchant for "passing a good time," the Native Americans who occupied South Louisiana were having a good time of their own. Of the indigenous tribes, Nancy Friedman observes, "Native Americans indulged in elaborate dances, spirited gambling, stickball games . . . Europeans adopted these and added billiards, duels, promenades and horse racing" (27). This happy marriage of multicultural hedonism multiplied over the centuries with several cultures (Spanish, Irish, German, Italian, African, Haitian, Cuban, Croatian, Vietnamese, etc.) each making its own intemperate contribution and continues to this day.

In the eighteenth century, public balls were held twice a week and were attended by virtually everyone. Dancing, eating, drinking, and gambling were the main events. Dressing to the nines was the norm. Dressing up remains an integral part of entertainment in New Orleans to this day.

So important were these weekly balls to the natives that when France ceded Louisiana to Spain, the primary concern was not the political or economic implications of the transfer of state but whether or not the Spanish Crown would discontinue the weekly parties. The French colonists took no chances. Not long after the first Spanish Colonial governor arrived in town in 1768, he was promptly shanghaied, deposited onto an outbound ship and told not to come back. By the time Napoleon Bonaparte sold out to Thomas Jefferson, New Orleans had well established itself as a party town and maintained a detached indifference to whatever flag was flying in Jackson Square.

So if New Orleans has resisted American mores so successfully, why has its gay past remained so closeted? For that we can thank two institutions: the Roman Catholic Church and good old fashioned greed. Make no mistake about it; at its core, New Orleans is a Catholic city. And while Roman Catholicism is relatively permissive compared to its Protestant counterparts, it has always toed the line on homosexuality. In the Prohibition Era, homophobia existed for sure, but given New Orleans' carefree live and let live attitude, such homophobia probably existed more because it had to rather than for any real fear or hatred in the hearts of people. In other words, if the Catholic Church didn't condemn homosexuality so venomously, it's reasonable to assume most New Orleanians would have adopted a much more *laissez faire* attitude toward gayness—out of sight, out of mind; don't ask, don't tell, as it were. That's not to say gay life would have been any more visible, though. In *Madame Vieux Carré,* Scott Ellis argues that tourism—more specifically, the money tourists bring to the city—provided a strong incentive to keep gays in the closet (67). That gay people had plenty of money to spend never occurred to the power structure that ran the city. The spending power of the gay community wasn't realized until the late 1980s.

To be sure, the law hindered tolerance. Before and after Prohibition, a city ordinance forbade bar owners from serving "degenerates" and doing so could result in a police raid. Gay bars, as we know them now, did not, indeed, could not, legally exist. A few bars, however, welcomed gays. One such bar was Café Lafitte, located on the corner of Bourbon and St. Phillip Streets.

In Exile

One Gay Man's Vision for the Vieux Carré

IF SEXUAL IDENTITY AND NOTIONS OF GENDER ARE SOCIALLY CONSTRUCTED, as Foucault insisted they are, there was very little construction going on prior to the advent of gay bars in the United States. The closet was not only a linguistic metaphor but also a very real, very invisible material space. Much has been written about the burgeoning gay communities of New York and San Francisco at the turn of the twentieth century, but the queers in New Orleans have been largely ignored among gay historians. Their closet remained quiet and crowded. Considering the fact there isn't a lot of source material to work with and, to a lesser extent, the subtle anti-Southern bias in much of American historiography, the neglect of New Orleans in American gay history narratives is somewhat explainable, if regrettable.

One thing New York, San Francisco, and New Orleans have in common is they are all ports of entry to the United States for international visitors and immigrants. As major ports, all three cities host large, transient populations. Gay historians have long noted the effect of such demographics on the gay community. Charles Kaiser, for example, argues in *The Gay Metropolis* that the modern gay liberation movement in the United States can be traced to the enlisted men who traveled the globe in World War II:

> People from all over the country who had assumed that they were unique learned that they were not alone. Soldiers and sailors also got a chance to sample gay culture all over the world— and discovered that large gay communities already existed in American ports of entry like San Francisco and New York City (xii).

Kaiser does not mention a gay community in New Orleans perhaps because unlike New York or San Francisco, gay life in New Orleans was not concentrated in a specific neighborhood. In the opening years of the twentieth century, San Francisco had its Tenderloin District and New York had its Greenwich Village, but New Orleans had no gayborhood. In the present day, we can point to the Marigny and lower Quarter as "gay zones," but at the dawn of the century, the Marigny was home to a low income, working class of people and the Quarter was essentially a run-down slum housing mostly Sicilian immigrants.

In the nineteenth century, sections of the Quarter were well established "sex zones." As was the case in most port cities, the waterfront was where many sex workers congregated. Gallatin Street running along the French Market was particularly seedy. Lucy J. Fair observes the waterfront entertained "an usually high number of Greek seafarers . . . Such Greek bars even today remain heavily mixed, straight and gay" (893). In the early twentieth century, Storyville (where the Iberville Housing Project now stands) was the city's primary red-light district although lower Canal Street and the Exchange Place Alley area was also the working domain of many hustlers and prostitutes.[8]

The Quarter began to evolve from slum to artist's enclave in 1915 with the arrival in the Vieux Carré of Lyle Saxon. Saxon, himself a gay man, was a tireless advocate for the French Quarter by leading key restoration efforts and successfully attracting a plethora of writers and artists to the neighborhood. Saxon was a visionary who, more than anyone else of his time, realized the intangible quality of the Quarter that would later be described as artistic inspiration.

Saxon knew that to be in New Orleans is to step outside of time and enter a world of dreams and letters, a world perfumed by jasmine and oleander with the faintest hint of mud scent wafting in from the Mississippi, a world where people move slowly, aware of but unconcerned with time. He knew that in New Orleans, especially the Quarter, myth and reality meld to

---

[8] Storyville was a thirty-eight block area where prostitution was legal from 1897 to 1917. Even today this area (Iberville to Canal, Royal to S. Peters) houses the Quarter's sole adult bookstore with attendant peep show stalls, a few brothels masquerading as Oriental Spas, and some of the Quarter's sleaziest strip joints.

form a dreamy realm where imagination reigns supreme and care is wholly abandoned. For artists and dreamers, the city herself *is* a poem. New Orleans has been described as the longest running literary salon in America and it really is true. Andrei Codrescu writes of New Orleans:

> I had the fleeting thought that everyone, dead or alive, returns to New Orleans. If people can't come back in their lifetimes, they come back when they are dead. And everyone who ever lived here, the costumed French and Spanish dandies, the Victorian ladies of Kate Chopin's age, the whores and ruffians, and the poets, are still here. In a city like New Orleans, built for human beings in the age before cars, it's possible to move about the streets with ease and there is plenty of room for everyone" (61).

Albert Einstein famously observed imagination was more important than knowledge. What he meant is that knowledge is often conjured from imagination. Such was certainly the case in his famous thought experiments. He imagined what it would be like to travel at the speed of light and when he quit daydreaming, humanity had a revolutionary new understanding of physics and the universe and our place in it.

But imagination spawns much more than knowledge; from imagination springs art and music and literature and food, to say nothing of hopes and dreams and the occasional nightmare. If there was ever a place on earth that embraces imagination and the creativity it engenders, that place is New Orleans. It is no wonder jazz and gumbo were born here or that no other American city has a Carnival season culminating in Mardi Gras. It's no wonder the streets here are named after chefs and musicians and mythological figures, including all the Muses. More than one observer has described New Orleans as a far-flung outpost of the Hellenistic world so it is no surprise the Muses feel at home in this New World Mount Parnassus. Their interplay charges the atmosphere with creativity and fills the air with inspiration.

Lyle Saxon knew it and preached it, redeeming and transforming the Quarter in the process. In so doing, he in effect carved out a "gay space" in a city where no such space previously existed. The first tangible manifestation of that space was Café Lafitte in Exile. Eventually, the bar would become the loci of the gay gentrification of the lower Quarter.[9] Saxon became very good friends with Café Lafitte's original owners, especially Mary Collins.[10] Not much is known about Collins' life or how she met Saxon.

Saxon's legacy lives on not only in the Quarter but also in the neighboring Marigny for he bequeathed his passion for preservation to future generations of gay men.[11] The gay men who revitalized the Marigny in the 1970s and 1980s may rightfully claim Saxon's mantle, and he would certainly approve of the Marigny's bohemian character. In "The Gay Penchant for Preservation," Will Fellows explores what drives

---

[9] The word "gentrification" requires some explanation. The word often has negative connotations that conjure images of class assertion and displacement of lower income groups. This issue becomes problematic in the evolution of "gayborhoods" because gays themselves are a traditionally marginalized group. Some reject the term gentrification and prefer "historical preservation." For our purposes, the word gentrification simply refers to a neighborhood with a high number of gay residents and/or businesses. For more on the gay gentrification versus historical preservation debate we refer the reader to: Brown-Saracino's "Social Preservationists and the Quest for Authenticity," Bryant's *Flag Wars*, Byrne's *Two Cheers for Gentrification*, Fellows' *A Passion to Preserve*, Glatzer and Westmoreland's *Quinceanera*, Knopp's "Some Theoretical Considerations of Gay Involvement in an Urban Land Market," and Zukin's "Gentrification: Culture and Capital in the Urban Core."

[10] In his seminal work, the autobiographical *The Friends of Joe Gilmore*, Saxon devotes a chapter to Mary Collins. Collins was gay.

[11] The gay gentrification of the Marigny is an integral part of the history of gay New Orleans and is explored at length in an unpublished dissertation by Lawrence M. Knopp, Jr., entitled "Gentrification and Gay Community Development in a New Orleans Neighborhood." The complete dissertation is available in the Williams Research Center of The Historic New Orleans Collection.

the extraordinary gay male penchant for preservation? He writes:

> The typical facile explanations tend to revolve around things like gay men's disposable income, childlessness, social oppression and marginalization. In reality, I discovered a rather consistent pattern comprising five key traits.
>
> > Gender Atypicality: Blend of masculine and feminine sensibilities and values.
> >
> > Domophilia: Great love of houses and things homey; a deep domesticity.
> >
> > Romanticism: Relating to the past in imaginative and emotional ways.
> >
> > Aestheticism: Extraordinary visual understanding and design-mindedness.
> >
> > Connection- and Continuity-Mindedness: Valuing a sense of flowing history and a relationship to the lives and possessions of those who have gone before.

This analysis rings true and it makes sense. "A deep domesticity," "relating to the past in imaginative and emotional ways," "a relationship to the lives . . . who have gone before": do not all these characteristics emanate from a profound yearning for belonging? This yearning is a ghost that hauntingly defined what it meant to be gay in pre-Stonewall America, and it's a specter that is still conjured every time a young schoolboy realizes he is "different." Thanks to Saxon and those who inherited his vision, it's a phantom that is nowhere near as scary as it used to be.

Part One - Pre 1960: The Closet Door Creaks

The creation of gay enclaves within larger cities certainly has its advantages for the gay community, namely safe and visible spaces for gays to be themselves; however, the gay neighborhood may also have its disadvantages. Some sociologists have questioned the value of safe spaces for minority populations. Exploring the African-American experience, Farah Jasmine Griffin writes of ghettos:

> At their most progressive . . . spaces of retreat, healing and resistance; at their most reactionary . . . potentially provincial spaces which do not encourage resistance but instead help create complacent subjects whose only aim is to exist within the confines of the power that oppresses them (9).

Is Griffin's warning applicable to the "gayification" of the lower Quarter and Marigny? Yes and no. At the time, gays had accepted their oppression as a sad fact of life. Resistance was a difficult concept to grasp, and given the *milieu* in which they found themselves, just having a "gay" area was a giant leap forward.

Bourbon Street Gets Its First Gay Bar

IN 1933, TOMMY CAPLINGER, HAROLD BARTELL, AND MARY COLLINS opened Café Lafitte. They were accepting of and welcoming to their gay clientele and offered them a safe place to drink and socialize. Although the bar could not be classified a "gay bar" as we think of that term today, it was as gay friendly as the times would permit.[12] And, as one might expect, it was a trendy

---

[12] Notions of sexual identity and orientation did not exist in America until the advent of the gay rights movement, traditionally thought of as beginning with Stonewall in 1969. The seeds of the movement had been planted years earlier with Alfred Kinsey's *Sexuality in the Human Male* (1948), the founding of the Mattachine Society (1950) and the founding of the Daughters of Bilitis (1955), but it was not until the Stonewall Riot (1969) that the gay community became visible on a national scale. In the previous

nightspot. Robert Kinney mentions the bar in his classic 1942 book *The Bachelor in New Orleans* suggesting, "If the bartender is passed out, go behind the bar and mix your own drink!" (28).

In a city known for its bars, Café Lafitte's was a must stop for visitors and a Mecca for celebrities. In *My New Orleans*, local culinary legend Ella Brennan recalls the scene at Café Lafitte in the 1940s and 1950s:

> Café Lafitte attracted all of the great talents in town. Tennessee Williams could be found there every night he was in town. You might run into the lead dancer for the Ballet Russes or a film star or actors in a hit play or the fabulous Mexican sculptor Enrique Alferez or politicians such as Hubert Humphrey and Eugene McCarthy or local politicos such as Earl Long and Chep Morrison or famous authors and syndicated journalists such as Robert Rouark (62).

Caplinger, Bartell, and Collins were generous too, freely running bar tabs for those who had no money. Eighteen years after the end of Prohibition, John Barbe the owner of the building died and his estate put the building up for auction. The bar owners could not afford to purchase it, and when the building sold, the bar closed for a few months. When it reopened, under the new ownership of John T. Moore, the bar's gay clientele were no longer welcome. Caplinger, Bartell, and Collins signed a lease on another building on the same block, opened another bar and called it Café Lafitte in Exile,

---

decades, homosexuality was conceived of in terms of acts, not being— something that is done, not a state of existence. After the decline of Gallatin Street as a sex zone, gays were relegated to a few straight bars that didn't forbid their patronage but were less than welcoming, notably a speakeasy in the lower Pontalba Apartment Building and two bars that catered to African-Americans, the Golden Feather on St. Bernard Avenue and the Dream Castle on Frenchman Street.

the word "exile" referring to their gay patrons who were "in exile" from the former bar. Years later, at the original bar, a box full of unpaid bar tabs was found, the sum of which would have paid for the building many times over.

Caplinger, who was straight, became something of a legend in the French Quarter not only as a brilliant bar owner but also for his generosity toward Quarterites, artists, writers, and anyone down on his luck. When he died in 1956, *The New Orleans States-Item* ran a glowing obituary article chronicling his contributions to the Vieux Carré and every bar on Bourbon Street honored him by briefly dimming their lights and observing a moment of silence.[13]

The original location of Café Lafitte (now called Lafitte's Blacksmith Shop) has an interesting history of its own—at least the building does.[14] The structure was built sometime between 1772 and 1791 by Nicolas Touze and is widely considered to be the oldest building used as a bar in the United States. The architectural style of the building is old French Provincial Louis XV or *Briquette-Entre-Poteauxe*, common in Louisiana under French rule. Between 1772 and 1791, the building was owned by Captain Rene Beluche, a privateer whose ship "Spy" was a member of Jean Lafitte's Barataria fleet. For this reason, it is generally thought the Blacksmith Shop was a front for Lafitte's smuggling operations in the city.[15] In the late 1700s, two fires destroyed much of the French Quarter, but the Blacksmith Shop was spared primarily because of its slate roofing. Ironically, because Louisiana was under Spanish rule at the time of the fires, much of the architecture in the French Quarter is actually Spanish. The Blacksmith Shop remains a favorite haunt among locals and tourists alike. Gay folk, though, are no longer a regular fixture; the regular crowd now

---

[13] Griffin, Thomas. "Padlocked Door Tells Story." *New Orleans States-Item* 27 March 1956.

[14] The following information is taken from the Lafitte's Blacksmith Shop website: http://www.lafittesblacksmithshop.com/AboutUs.html

[15] There is no historical evidence to support this claim.

is decidedly straight.

The opposite end of the block is not so straight. Café Lafitte in Exile opened in its current incarnation at 901 Bourbon in 1953. The grand opening was celebrated with a costume party. To avoid being discovered and raided, the front door was barricaded with sandbags and barbed wire. Those in the know had to enter through the back door. One legend holds that on the night Café Lafitte in Exile opened, several regulars from the old location met there, had a few drinks, and then in unison stood up, picked up their barstools and marched down the street to the new location—an act not only of defiance, but also a rather dramatic coming out declaration. Imbibing gays of the day may have been in exile, but at least they had a bar of their own. It was the first predominantly gay bar in New Orleans.

Before it became Café Lafitte, the building at 901 Bourbon was a grocery store. At that time, the structure had no balcony and no stucco; the wood walls were painted yellow. The interior was remodeled for bar service, the two most notable renovations being the shape of the bar and the introduction of the eternal flame, both of which were designed to reflect the shape of the Mississippi River as it flows around the city. Enrique Alferez ("Ricky" to his friends) who had been a regular at Café Lafitte's designed both. In the early days, there was a liquor rack behind the bar in the same shape and a foot rail around the fountain where people could sit and place their drinks on the edge of the fountain, which sprayed water out of its three corners.

Alferez, a Mexican born Louisiana artist, initially gained fame fighting with Pancho Villa in the Mexican Revolution. He came to New Orleans in 1929 and had an illustrious career as an accomplished sculptor whose works adorn City Park, the Lakefront Airport, and many buildings throughout the Central Business District. He was one of many artists that frequented Lafitte's. Alferez died in 1999 at the age of 95.

The story behind the eternal flame, like much of the history of the bar—indeed, New Orleans herself—is shrouded in mystery and mythology. One common story claims the flame is a memorial to the original regular crowd's (and by extension, future generations of drinking gays) status as "exiles." Alferez never claimed that was what he had in mind when he gifted the artwork to the bar, but who knows? It makes for a nice story. In the early years, the flame also served as a fountain but that function ceased when drunken barflies began using it as a urinal. A later owner of the bar declared the flame was a tribute to arson—arson that enabled him and his lover to buy Café Lafitte's. The story goes that they set fire to their former business in another state and used the insurance money to buy Lafitte's.

Early photographs of the bar, dating from the mid-1950s, reveal a wooden structure with no balcony. Where the balcony now stands was flimsy looking awning with no support beams. The two side doors on Bourbon Street opposite the Clover Grill are closed and shuttered. On the frame of the main door overlooking the intersection of Bourbon and Dumaine, in vertical letters, are the words CAFÉ LAFITTE IN EXILE. Next to the main door, facing Bourbon, are two small signs, which are illegible in the picture. To the left of the main door, on Dumaine, is another door. A photograph from 1962 suggests a paint job and the addition of a firebox on the corner of the intersection. The lettering of the sign is also changed. Also, window air condition units have been added to the upstairs. The two small sides on the Bourbon façade are gone.

By the late 1950s, the bar was under the ownership of Tommy Hopkins, who lived in an upstairs apartment where the balcony bar now is. By all accounts, Hopkins, who was straight, was a thoroughly decent man who harbored no prejudices and went out of his way to make people feel welcome. Charlie the cab driver, a friend of Hopkins and one of the few regulars from the 1950s still around, recalls the atmosphere of the bar, "It was a place where you could talk, where you could be yourself." He also recalls meeting Ernest Hemmingway in the bar, "a total drunk who would talk your ear off, usually about politics."

In the 1950s and 1960s, Café Lafitte, was the premiere gay bar in New Orleans. Albert Carey, who became a regular in the 1960s, describes Café Lafitte in those days as "a cocktail party to which you were always invited." Albert recalls meeting Truman Capote and Tennessee Williams there in the early 1970s:

> In those days I lived on Bourbon and frequented Lafitte's. One evening I saw Truman Capote sitting at the bar talking with someone. I approached him and said, "I don't mean to come on to you but I've always admired your work. May I buy you a drink?" And he responded, "Only if you sit and have one with us." He was so sweet, not at all bitchy like some have said. He even signed a beverage napkin for me. Another time I saw Tennessee Williams standing by the flame. As I neared him I could see he was very, very drunk but I introduced myself anyway. He gave me a very limp handshake, like a dead fish, and mumbled something incoherently, which kind of grossed me out, and he almost fell down in the process.

Also in the 1950s and 1960s, women and African Americans were not allowed in the bar, with few exceptions. This began to change around 1970 but even well into the 1970s, women were required to produce multiple forms of identification before entering. Lesbian Clay Latimer laughingly remembers that was not a problem for her because "they thought I was a boy." One tactic the bar employed to keep lesbians out was to require women to wear dresses. For the most part, this strategy effectively maintained the bar's tradition of men only. It wasn't until the mid 1990s that women were permitted in the bar without having to produce multiple forms of identification.

Post War Gay New Orleans

AS AMERICA SETTLED INTO A DECADE OF DENIAL and invisibility for anyone who wasn't a straight, white, Christian male, a gay subculture began to emerge that would eventually challenge the very notions of *Ozzie and Harriet* "normalcy" that defined the 1950s.

Reminiscing on the gay scene in New Orleans in the 1950s, Charlie summed up his feelings by saying the gay community was much more close-knit then because it had to be. Although a handful of gay bars were in competition with each other, the bar owners communicated with each other and took a genuine interest in their clientele, often bailing them out of jail after raids or lending money to regulars who fell on hard times. In one memorable incident decades later, the police raided the Bourbon Pub and made several arrests. Owner Jerry Menefee bonded everyone out, had cabs waiting at the jail to return them to the bar, and then gave them free drinks for the rest of the night. Underage drinking in the 1950s was common and permitted primarily because the older gays knew all too well what it was like to be queer at sixteen or seventeen years old in a very straight world. Of course, bailing your customers out of jail and young eye candy was good for business, but beyond that, there was a bona-fide sense of camaraderie across the community—a sense which has diminished considerably in these out-and-proud times.

For much of the mid-twentieth century, gay life in New Orleans was centered in the Quarter in a few bars and in the homes of a few artists, writers, and photographers. In 1939, jazz musician "Miss Dixie" Fasnacht[16] opened Dixie's Bar of Music in the downtown business district and in 1949 moved the bar to the Quarter. According to Roberts Batson, she may be the model for a character in Gore Vidal's *The City and the Pillar* (1948). Although she retired in 1964, Miss Dixie, who died in 2011 at the age of 101, remains a legend, especially for

---

[16] Born Yvonne Fasnacht, Miss Dixie, in addition to her contribution to gay history in New Orleans, became a something of a minor legend in the history of Jazz. An accomplished clarinetist, she traveled in the 1930s with several all-girl bands including, *The Harmony Maids, The Smart Set, Sophisticates of Swing,* and *The Southland Rhythm Girls.* Interestingly, Dixie's last name, Fasnacht, is the Swiss-German term for Mardi Gras (Eve of Fasting).

her support of her patrons, who were frequently harassed by police during periodic "clean up" campaigns. Hoyle A. Byrd, Jr. remembers the first time he went to Ms. Dixie's at the tender age of sixteen:

> I was nervous and Dixie must have seen it because she made me feel welcome and had me sit by the register, which was near the staircase, next to her sister who was the cashier. She told me if the place was raided, I could go upstairs and hide. She was the sweetest lady.

For a brief time, there was also The Starlet Lounge and Tony Bacino's Bar. The city's first lesbian-themed bars were on the Tchoupitoulas Street waterfront in the 1950s but these were short-lived. In addition to Café Lafitte and Dixie's Bar of Music, both in the Quarter, the famous transvestite club the My-O-My, which flourished during the 1940s and 1950s, was located on the lakefront, and across town on St. Claude there was The Golden Feather, a bar that catered to African-American gay men[17]. There were also a few lesbian bars on Tchoupitoulas near the Irish Channel (Fair 895).[18] Outside the bars, gay life manifested itself in private cocktail parties (one thinks of Dorian Greene's Peace Party soiree in John Kennedy Toole's *A Confederacy of Dunces*) and homes such as Lyle Saxon's literary salon on Royal Street and the home of famed lesbian photographer Francis Benjamin Johnston. Batson writes:

> Johnston retired to New Orleans in 1940 after she completed her final large project, a photographic documentation of Southern architecture. She

---

[17] Club My-O-My featured live shows with a band and usually six female impersonators per performance. Jimmy Calloway, Master of Ceremonies for thirty years, recalls the club drew celebrities from time to time including Carmen Miranda, Howard Hughes, and New York mobster Frank Costello.

[18] In this article, Fair mentions the lesbian bars on Tchopitoulas but does not name them.

lived in the city until her death in 1952. Her partner, a younger woman named Tom Sawyer, survived Johnston by three decades . . . And native New Orleanian Truman Capote, who returned to his birthplace in 1945, where, holed up in his apartment at 711 Royal Street, he wrote the bulk of his first major work, *Other Voices, Other Rooms* (1948). He later called that period, "the freest time of my life."

In the 1960s and 1970s, lesbian pioneer Alice Brady owned and operated a number of lesbian bars on North Rampart.

In 1949, Bob Demmons founded The Lundi Gras Luncheon, the oldest continuing non-bar-related activity in the New Orleans gay community. And in 1953, The Steamboat Club, the oldest gay social organization in New Orleans, was founded. For a time, The Steamboat Club met upstairs at Café Lafitte when it housed the short-lived restaurant, The Streetcar. In recent years, The Steamboat Club has held its Lundi Gras luncheon in an upstairs dining room at Arnaud's. Since 1999, the group has held its Thursday before Mardi Gras party at the Balcony Bar at Lafitte's.

The first gay Carnival club, the Krewe of Yuga (KY), began in 1958 and was founded as a lark, a party spoofing traditional society balls. (This satirical genesis echoes the founding of the Zulu Social Aid and Pleasure Club fifty years earlier, which began as a spoof of Rex, the King of Carnival). Yuga flourished until a police raid of their 1962 ball abruptly destroyed it. In an incredible lapse of public relations judgment, Yuga had chosen a private school as the sight of their ball.

There were also unwritten rules and an understood protocol governing gay life in the 1950s and 1960s. More often than not, bartenders served as the arbiters and enforcers of this code of conduct. Hustlers, for example, were relegated to a few bars in the upper Quarter, most notably Wanda's on Iberville and Mom's Society Page (where several bartenders were ex-priests) in Exchange Place Alley, and had to operate under the watchful eyes of the bartenders. The same was true for Johns. Rarely did hustler and John negotiate directly; rather, the bartender brokered such transactions, acting as advisor and referee to both parties.

The Pink Menace

SURREPTITIOUS CODES WERE NECESSARY FOR 1950S GAY AMERICA, and especially in New Orleans, which was much more homophobic than recent generations can possibly imagine. Despite New Orleans' penchant for tolerance and its *laissez faire* attitude, gays in New Orleans have always faced a considerable amount of homophobia, especially from police. Although police harassment of gay bars now is mainly a thing of the past, it was, nonetheless, a very ugly past. Many bar owners, especially ones working with and for the mafia, paid the police to leave them alone. The manager of a local restaurant recalls that when he was a regular at Café Lafitte in the 1960s, a police officer would come in each week like clockwork and collect an envelope stuffed with cash.[19] Tom Wood stopped making the payments when he took over and eventually obtained a restraining order against the police because of their harassment. Nevertheless, the vice squad would, on occasion, either raid bars or send undercover cops (almost always young and good-looking ones) into the bars to make arrests. This practice continued well into the 1970s. Albert Carey remembers meeting a good looking young man at the bar who was an undercover police officer. "When he excused himself to go to the bathroom, the bartender told me to be careful because he was a vice cop." Bartenders customarily slapped a wooden board on the bar to warn patrons they were getting too touchy-feely. Arrests were often accompanied by a beating and pressure to name other "perverts." Anyone unfortunate enough to be arrested for "crimes against nature" or "committing a

---

[19] Several men we interviewed are convinced that some gay bars were owned by the mafia. This may be the case but it is more likely that bars made payments to the mafia in order to secure not only its protection but also protection from the police, with whom it had a symbiotic relationship.

lewd act" had his name and picture published in *The Times Picayune*. Often this resulted in family alienation, loss of a job, and, in some cases, loss of a place to live. This type of harassment began to subside in the 1980s.

In 1955, Police Superintendent Provosty A. Dayries publicly proclaimed that homosexuals were the city's "Number One vice problem," adding, "They are the ones we want to get rid of most."[20] Widespread ignorance and familiar stereotypes of gay people were prevalent, especially the notion that homosexuals were predatory and looking to recruit teenagers and children. In 1951, *The Times-Picayune* ran a story entitled, "Curb Advocated on Homosexuals: Crackdown to Save Young Persons Demanded":

> A warning that homosexuals in the French Quarter are at work corrupting high school boys and girls was made Friday by Richard R. Foster, chairman of the Mayor's Committee on the Vieux Carré, in an address before the Civic Council of New Orleans.
>
> For that reason, he said, the homosexual problem is one of the city's most serious. "In several instances, parents have come to police begging them to save their children," he asserted.
>
> High school boys and girls enticed into places habituated by homosexuals often see an obscene show or something of that nature as a starter," he added.
>
> The homosexuals are, he said, "continuously recruiting" and there are at least four "places" in the Quarter which cater to almost no one but homosexuals.
>
> "It almost seems as if youngsters who develop homosexual tendencies in other Southern cities are put on a train and sent to New Orleans," he

---

[20] "Dayries Cites No. 1 Vice Problem" *Times-Picayune* 30 June 1955.

said.[21]

About a month earlier, *The Times-Picayune* ran another article along the same lines with a new twist. At a meeting of the Mayor's Advisory Committee, Chairman Foster argued that the city should develop a strategy for discouraging "perverts" (emphasis ours) from coming to New Orleans, claiming most homosexuals in New Orleans were "out-of-towners."[22] That gay people lived in New Orleans was either incomprehensible or too distasteful to bear. The level of denial and clueless-ness revealed in the article rivals the level of bigotry and hatred permeating straight society at the time. One man we interviewed noted, "We never flaunted our sexuality then because we were so afraid."

In 1958, the white-male-Christian-heterosexual establishment adopted a more pragmatic approach in their crusade to save the city from the "pink menace." In that year, the city council established a "Committee on the Problem of Sex Deviates." An initial report of the committee proposed a "climate of hostility"[23] be adopted toward homosexuals (as if the climate was not hostile enough). As its chairman, the council appointed Jacob Morrison, a prominent citizen and co-founder of the Vieux Carré Property Owners and Associates. Morrison had been a thorn in the side of the gay community for years. He had a few years earlier led a successful effort to have The Starlet Lounge's (at the corner of Chartres and St. Phillip) liquor license revoked, and then turned his attention to Tony Bacino's bar on Toulouse (where The Dungeon, a straight, heavy-metal bar, now is). In the summer of 1958, the manager and staff of Tony Bacino's were arrested six times. They were charged with violating this remarkable city ordinance: *"No person of lewd, immoral, or dissolute character, sexual*

[21] "Curb Advocated on Homosexuals: Crackdown to Save Young Persons Demanded." *Times-Picayune* 28 Apr. 1951.

[22] "Vieux Carre Unit Seeks Ordinance." *Times-Picayune* 8 March 1951.

[23] "Program is Up to City Council." *Times-Picayune* 26 Oct. 1958.

pervert . . . shall be employed . . ." in bars and restaurants.[24] Amazingly, this ordinance was not repealed until 1993. After the last arrest, the manager and bartenders of Tony Bacino's filed for, and were awarded, an injunction and temporary restraining order. Ultimately they lost the case.

As is often the case when extreme rhetoric couples with profound ignorance, violence ensued. In 1958, three Tulane students (John S. Farrell, Alberto A. Calvo, and David P. Drennan) decided to go to the Quarter to "roll a queer."[25] The three undergrads proceeded down Bourbon Street to Café Lafitte. Farrell entered the bar around 1:30 in the morning while Calvo and Drennan waited outside. In the bar, Farrell met 26-year-old Fernando Rios. The two men decided to "hook-up" and left the bar together. Farrell and Rios entered Pirate's Alley when Farrell began physically assaulting Rios. Calvo and Drennan, who were waiting in the alley, joined the attack. Rios, after being struck in the head several times and kicked repeatedly in the abdomen, died at Charity Hospital of a fractured skull about twelve hours after being discovered in the Alley around 6:15 a.m.

During a routine autopsy, the city coroner discovered the victim had an unusually thin cranium. Farrell, Calvo, and Drennan were arrested and charged with murder. The trial began on January 21, 1959. At trial, the defendants admitted to the beating but argued he died because of his "eggshell cranium," not because of their attack. Tortured logic aside, this defense made perfect sense to a homophobic, all male, all white jury in mid-twentieth century New Orleans and the three students were easily acquitted after deliberating a mere two hours and fifteen minutes.[26]

---

[24] Section 5-66,CCS 18, 537. For more on the repeal of this ordinance, see note 64 on page 260 of Scott S. Ellis' *Madame Vieux Carre*.

[25] Rickey, Robert. "Murder in Pirate's Alley." Unpublished Paper. New Orleans Public Library.

[26] For those interested in more information on the attack and subsequent trial, see "Murder in Pirate's Alley," an unpublished paper by Robert Rickey in the New Orleans Public Library.

The acquittal and attendant press coverage of the trial provide a glimpse into the highly homophobic public attitudes toward "queers" at the time. When the "not guilty" verdict was announced, the courtroom erupted in applause and cheers for the jury.[27] The *New Orleans States-Item* featured on its front page a picture of the defendants smiling broadly next to a boxed joke entitled "Today's Chuckle" which read, "Overheard in a night club: ordinarily I never chase a man, but this one was getting away." The District Attorney's office filed robbery charges against the three students, but that charge was reduced to theft and the judge sentenced Farrell and Drennan to six months (Calvo had returned to his native Panama). The judge (George Platt) then immediately suspended the sentence. Throughout the ordeal, a deluge of letters poured into the editorial offices of the city's newspapers, the overwhelming majority of them supporting the gay-bashing murderers and calling on the city to "clean up the Quarter." The few letters in support of gays were often backhanded. One incensed reader argued that police should leave the gay bars alone so the "perverts" wouldn't feel compelled to mingle with "normal" people.

---

[27] "Jury Acquits 3 Students Tried in Slaying of Guide." *Times-Picayune* 24 Jan. 1959.

Part Two
The 1960s: The Closet Door Inches Open

THE 1960S WAS A PERIOD OF GROWTH and development for gay New Orleans, a season of building upon the foundations laid in previous decades. It was during this era that gay culture in New Orleans first began to resemble what it has become today. We may think of this period as childhood with Café Lafitte in Exile fulfilling the role of nurturing mother. In this section, we look at the factors that played a key role in the formation of a gay identity and highlight the early incarnations of that identity.

Part Two - The 1960s: The Closet Door CInches Open

The Centrality of the Gay Bar and the Chameleon Syndrome

BACK IN THE DECADES when most closet doors were firmly shut, and long before the Internet was a twinkle in Al Gore's eye, the role of the gay bar was monumental in the lives of gay men. It is difficult for young, say under thirty, Friends of Dorothy to imagine a world with no social/sex networking sites, no gay characters on television (or gay-themed television shows for that matter), no cars with rainbow stickers. The threat of being arrested merely for *being* gay is utterly incomprehensible to them. They never knew a world where gayness was invisible.

But that world did exist. It was a world of darkness for gay men, a world where their core beings were hidden. It was a world of pretense, of false realities and double lives. In such a world, the gay bar afforded these men the only opportunity to be themselves, to let the light shine, if only for a few hours, on their true identities.

Identity in general is a complicated thing; for the gay man doubly so; for the closeted, even more complex still. We all assume various and sometimes competing identities: son, father, husband, employee, co-worker, friend, etc. For the straight man, negotiating the tensions that accompany multiple identities is manageable because his external world is permeated with examples and reference points. But for a young gay man who doesn't know what the word "gay" means, an adolescent who lives in a society where homosexuality doesn't exist except in clinical psychiatric textbooks on mental disorders and in hushed whispers at family reunions and vitriolic sermons on eternal damnation—what reference point does he have? The gay bar, of course.

The gay bar for decades served not only as refuge and playground for gay men who had grown comfortable in their roles as would-be outcast sodomites, but also as identity giver for those just coming to terms with their gayness. Clendinen and Nagourney describe gay bars before gay visibility this way: "If bars in the '60s still symbolized the rights of manhood to traditional young males, to young gay males trying to find the missing context of their lives, what a gay bar promised was much more: freedom, shelter, friendship, excitement, romance, seduction—escape" (17-18). For young and old alike, the gay bar was a safe space and a place for answers for those who felt the burgeoning yearnings of the identity that dare not speak its name.[28]

"Charlie Bear," a regular at Café Lafitte for forty-six years, grew up in a large family on Esplanade Avenue. As a kid, his parents, who were forward thinking, would take Charlie and his nine siblings walking along Bourbon Street and point out the strip clubs and the homosexual bars and other adult places they would face soon enough.

Charlie first went to Café Lafitte at the age of fifteen in 1964. At that time, the DJ booth didn't exist and that space was known as the "blow job corner." There, Charlie received his first blowjob by three older men he guesses must have been in their late twenties or thirty-something at the time. A few years later, Charlie went and fought in Vietnam, came home, married a woman, and had children. Divorced now and out to his children, Charlie is a fixture at the bar and credits Café Lafitte with helping him become comfortable with his sexuality.

Other men convey the same sentiment: that Café Lafitte provided them a reference point of what it means to be gay. This feeling is true for young and old alike, and they span the decades from the bar's inception to its current scene. Consider the story of Mike. Mike grew up in a small town in Pennsylvania where there was only one gay bar, which patrons had to enter through a back alley. When he came out to his brother, his brother's response was, "Move to New Orleans and never talk to me again." Not long afterwards, Mike's job as a traveling nurse brought him to New Orleans in 1997. Like so many visitors, he fell in love with New Orleans and never left. Mike, now forty-three, reports being shocked at how easy it was to be gay in New Orleans but was still fearful of discrimination and homophobia. He began making the rounds

---

[28] Bathhouses would later come into vogue in the 1970s. The oldest bathhouse in New Orleans, Club New Orleans, opened on Toulouse Street in 1973 and remains open today.

along "the fruit loop."[29] He describes Café Lafitte this way:

> This bar is different because it's more relaxed, comfortable. No one feels the need to pretend to be someone they're not. Lafitte's is my gay Cheers. Lafitte's helped me decide who I didn't want to be and molded who I became. Lafitte's is like New Orleans itself—always a character around, someone to talk to, always something to learn.

One thing Charlie Bear and Mike and countless others have learned is that being gay in a homophobic society means embracing the Chameleon Syndrome, that is, assuming a variety of identities which evolve over time. Indeed, time itself is a chameleon, constantly shuffling perspective like the multiple facets of the prism through which identity is viewed. Identity, and the cluster of meanings associated with it, is a gradually unfolding, multi-layered onion-riddle whose ultimate resolution comes with time.

John, a retired high school counselor on the subject of identity:

> I was more gay when I first came out than I am now. Being gay is just a small part of who I am. I grew up in Yazoo City, a small town in the Mississippi delta. My parents didn't even tell me I was Jewish until I was twelve or thirteen because the Klan was very active there at that time. And I didn't come to terms with my sexuality until I was thirty-one. I had been in therapy for about a year and during one session my psychiatrist simply told me, "You're gay" and it made sense. Growing up I had no exposure to gay people. Coming out was scary but fun.

---

[29] "The fruit loop" is a cluster of bars in the lower Quarter.

In Exile

Around that time I went to Germany to work in an American school. It was a one year assignment but I fell in love with Germany and ended up staying sixteen years. I hooked up with a lot of American soldiers over there. The gay scene in Germany is very open and the government pumps tons of money into the community like programs for confused teens. I guess they're trying to make up for the Holocaust. Anyway, after sixteen years I was ready to be an American again and so I came home. I chose New Orleans because I had been here before as a tourist and I figured New Orleans would work for me. I don't go out much anymore. Your energy and motivational levels change as you get older. Sometimes it's just easier to stay home and beat off.

If anything, Café Lafitte over the decades has (in addition to providing a place for gay men to get laid) provided a safe space, a refuge, if you will, from the Chameleon Syndrome. But the sanctuary of the gay bar may have had a negative consequence as well. Because gay bars afforded gay men one of the few opportunities to explore their sexuality (usually in the form of quasi-anonymous/quasi-public sex acts) and because those "crimes" were publicly exposed in newspapers following arrests, the stereotype that gay men are more promiscuous than straight men was born. Judith Butler, one of the founding luminaries of Queer Theory, observes, "There is no gender identity behind the expressions of gender . . . identity is performatively constituted by the very 'expressions' that are said to be its results" (Butler 25). Butler's claim is debatable but it certainly explains straight society's once prevailing view that gay men are obsessed with sex.[30]

---

[30] The primary tenet of Queer Theory is that identities are not fixed and do not determine who we are. This notion that identity is not connected to essence but rather to performance is, perhaps, its primary flaw and may explain why Queer Theory is no longer in vogue in the Humanities while the

Part Two - The 1960s: The Closet Door CInches Open

Every gay man sooner or later gets in touch with his inner-Dorothy and has at some point his "Toto Epiphany," that terrifying moment when he is confronted with the frightening realization that he is a faggot. We use that inflammatory word deliberately to convey the sense of dread and horror that often accompanies this recognition. Revulsion is only the beginning. What follows is mourning. And grieving. And sadness. And loss. Especially loss. Deep loss. Profound loss. Then acceptance, which gradually gives way to fulfillment.

I (Frank) recall my own "Toto Epiphany" occurring in college with a fraternity brother. Calvin and I were roommates and we were inseparable. But more than partners in crime, Calvin and I were lovers. Here is a journal entry from 2008:

> Calvin and I were fortunate in that we shared our "Toto, we're not in Kansas anymore" sacrament together. Most gay boys go through it terribly alone. Calvin and I shared the first steps of the glorious journey of identity discovery together. The first leg of that journey was shaded with the darkness that came from the deep fear and shame and self-loathing intrinsic to our well-guarded secret.
>
> Being out and proud was unthinkable to us then. On weekends, we would escape the closet and drive down to New Orleans from LSU. Lafitte's gave us a chance to not only be ourselves but also to catch a glimpse of the gay world. As our relationship grew, we each dealt with our gayness in radically different ways: he joined the Marines and felt all the more macho for it. I became a fundamentalist Christian and felt all the less sinful for it. Fortunately, his macho phase and my self-righteous phase didn't last long. But while they did, he went off to war and I

---

less theoretical field of Gay and Lesbian Studies continues to thrive in the Academy.

transferred to another school, but we did keep in touch for several years and from time to time meet in New Orleans to fuck and hang out at Lafitte's.

One of those occasions stands out in my memory. I had arrived in town before him and was waiting for him at the bar. I was sitting at the back point where the DJ booth now is when he came in. As soon as I saw him, I was reminded of Wordsworth's famous definition of poetry: "powerful feelings recollected in tranquility." Memories, and their accompanying emotions, began to surge. Not just the incredible, ineffable, unrepeatable euphoria of falling in love for the first time but also that untroubled spirit of youth—the dreams and hopes that lure us into young adulthood, the invincibility that reassures us we can do anything and never bothers to tell us we will one day die. How paradoxical to be so confidant yet lack so much experience!

I hadn't seen or heard from him in twelve years. Then, not long ago, he was in New Orleans for a few days and he contacted me. We met at Lafitte's and caught up with each other. He told me about his partner and he got to meet mine. Today Calvin is a psychiatrist and a gay rights advocate in San Francisco. As we left the bar, I briefly considered all the gifts time gives us if we accept them, the most generous of which, I think, is perspective.

A Lesbian's Perspective

RACHEL DANGERMOND is Director of Media and Business Development for one of the largest independent companies researching public companies for Wall Street investment firms. Rachel Dangermond in her own words:

I never thought about being gay or straight and

remember definitely having sexual feelings about a couple of women, not many, in my high school to college years. My best friend in high school was a masculine looking woman and right before we graduated she was spending the night at my house and we woke the next morning and she said, "You know I'm gay, right?" And I wasn't shocked, but surprised it had been articulated. There was a deep friendship between us and still is, however, what we laugh about now is when I told my mother my friend was gay, my mom said, "Oh my, how cosmopolitan!" That was in 1977. So I believe my mother's free spirit definitely lived inside of me. Then when I turned twenty, I moved back to New Orleans having lived in Atlanta and was dating an older man. We were at 4141, and he was a notorious cheat, and while I was in the bathroom, he left with another woman at the bar. The bartender was very sympathetic and offered to drive me home. She ended up seducing me and so began my dalliances with women sexually over the years. However, I never had a relationship with any of these women, only men, and I married three men for a total of twenty-one married years. While living in San Francisco, my mother, a widow, had a dalliance with a colleague that she shared with me. I was so thrilled for her that I sent her about five books on coming out that a gay friend there had told me about. My mom hid them and finally discreetly disposed of them!

I left San Francisco and came back after sixteen years and now live on Bayou St. John, in a community that is home to a larger than average percentage of lesbians as well as gays. On Fat Tuesday in 2008, I was waiting for St. Anne to arrive when I spotted a woman standing in front of Mimi's and it was love at first sight. We decided in five minutes to become Mardi Gras girlfriends and she moved in a week later and we adopted a child after two years, and now live in our predominantly lesbian community happy as clams. No one I know of has flinched about my becoming gay after fifty years, not in my family, not my colleagues, and not my friends. My eighty-year-old aunt said, "Well it was obvious men weren't working for you." My gay friends have marveled at this as many have not had similar support when they came out. I have young relatives and friends who have come to me about their own questions of sexuality and have heard many times from young people that our relationship is a model for what they hope to achieve in their life—a loving, stable family. I remember cautioning one young person who wanted to tell her parents right now that perhaps she might want to wait till after college because she might be gay till graduation and be in a highly experimental mode. Women tend to be much more fluid about their sexuality and even my most staunch lesbian friends have shared that they are attracted to the opposite sex.

When we travel in and out of the country, we looked for gay bars, yet here in New Orleans I'd say we rarely frequent gay-only bars. Our favorite restaurant is Meaux Bar and the proprietors and partners, Matt and Jim entertain a mixed crowd of locals, but it does have a nice slice of a New Orleans gay clientele. Frequently when we are traveling, we are propositioned by young men and it is curious that these men really believe we are "lacking" them in our life. One was as recent as our last trip abroad, in Morocco, a young man working in our guesthouse said he would just knock and we could let him in. Our sixteen-month-old child was with us. Because I've noticed in New York and other large cities how we, two women, are still a curiosity, it pains me to think of how difficult it must be for young women who are gay, who don't have other options, to come out and exist in this world where they remain other, different and queer still.

My partner is from Croatia, which is violently homophobic. I did not like that when I was there; having lived so long and then having partnered with a woman without batting my eye, to suddenly have to go in a closet I never lived in. It really discomforts me and caused stress in our relationship. It's easier for my partner because she grew up in this society, but it is very difficult for me. When we're there, we end up frequenting the nude beaches, which are much more gay friendly. However, last time we left Croatia, they were posting signs on beaches saying, "NO GAYS ALLOWED." It isn't a matter of being in the closet or not, it is a matter of safety— homosexuals are targets of violence in Croatia and it is best to travel there under the gaydar.

My dear friend from high school, who has been in a loving relationship for years now, told me one time to tell one of the young girls asking me about coming out "not to"; she said, "It's such a hard life. I wouldn't wish it on anyone." I felt sad for her and in general that my experience of being gay was not universal. My experience has been that gay life is much the same as the life of a free-spirited person, which is the model my mother offered me, particularly when she said, "You can be anything you want to be in your life." She was very supportive of my relationship with my partner and before it, my circle of friends that overindexed to gay. It certainly does not jive with what a dear friend's mother told her when she was young, "I wish you had told me you had cancer or some other disease."

I subscribe to the belief the world is changing. We are not perfect but we are making progress. We recently had a heterosexual young couple say they want to be like us when they grow up. That tells me we as a couple, as a family, transcend any vertical labeling and are perceived as universal. I would hope that would be the case everywhere very soon and I have faith in the youth of today it will happen. One thing I would tell any young person who is considering coming out is to not internalize homophobia. I believe that is the disease. And I would also tell women, probably more than men, to try to avoid labels, think of sexuality as fluid, as who you chose to be with as a personal choice, and to try to make your world on your terms.

Rachel's narrative raises some interesting questions: Is female sexuality more fluid than male sexuality? If so, how and why? Is the Kinsey scale truer for women than men? Are lesbians more resistant to labels than gay men? Is it better for gay youth in homophobic families to prolong coming out? What are the ethical and psychological implications of postponing the decision to come out? What about relationships where one party is out but the other is not? What is the best way to negotiate the tensions that inevitably arise from those relationships? Are the answers to these questions changing with the times?

Coming Out in the 1960s

IN 1965, JOHN TINSLEY was an undergraduate at LSU in Baton Rouge. During his sophomore year, he came out of the closet and moved off campus into a rental house with his gay friends. One day, a straight friend saw him hanging out with an obviously gay young man and promptly reported this disturbing news to the Dean of Men. John was called into the

Part Two - The 1960s: The Closet Door Clnches Open

Dean's office and gravely informed the university had compiled a dossier on him, specifically detailing his association with sexual deviates. He was also told he needed to move back on campus. "You need to get way from those people," the Dean informed him, adding, "If you move back on campus, this file goes away. If you don't, I'll tell your parents you're hanging around with queers." John recalls considering suicide:

> I almost jumped off the top of Tiger Stadium. I lost all my straight friends and my gay friends wanted nothing to do with me. I had become a pariah. Shortly after the episode, a straight friend from back home in Shreveport invited me to go to Mardi Gras in New Orleans. Once there, I managed to slip away from my straight friend and head to the gay bars. At Diogynes, I met Tommy. I ended up staying the entire weekend with him. We dated for a year and a half.
>
> I dropped out of school during the Vietnam war and went home to Shreveport. My brother-in-law told me I would be drafted but I told him I had nothing to worry about because I was gay. I trusted him not to tell my family but that was a mistake. After that I took a job in New Orleans and moved in with Tommy on St. Phillip Street in the Quarter. Well one day my aunt, who lived in the city, took me to dinner at T. Pittari's and told me my dad was coming down to New Orleans to kill Tommy and rescue me.
>
> My aunt, who was sympathetic but still confused by my gayness, agreed to meet Tommy and drove me back to the Quarter. As we approached St. Phillip, she spotted my father and M.S. Carroll, one of my family's political connections here, who ran in government, business, and political circles. I spotted them too, and they had guns. I later learned M.S. had the entire police force looking for me. My aunt talked

to them and told my father I didn't want to leave but my father was adamant, telling her, "We flew all the way down here to get him and we're not leaving without him." Reluctantly, I agreed to leave with them and we made our way to Moissant Airport. When I boarded the plane, I saw my grandmother waiting and I was so embarrassed. My brother-in-law had betrayed my trust.

Back in North Louisiana, I started seeing a psychiatrist—and planning my escape back to New Orleans. One weekend, while my family went to a party in New York, I stayed behind and caught a bus to New Orleans. At every stop along the way, I slinked down in the seat to hide, convinced that M.S. and the local sheriff would be waiting for me, ready to cart me off to the mental asylum. I finally made it to New Orleans and Tommy was waiting for me at the bus station. I had no contact with my family at first but after six months my dad, who was not a writer, sent me a letter saying he loved me. My family eventually realized my being gay was not a choice.

John eventually took a job in California and lived there thirty years. He recently moved back to New Orleans, noting, "The best memories of my life are in New Orleans."

Cruising

PUBLIC ATTITUDES IN THE 1950S had changed little in the 1960s. Because gays were forced to live in the closet, cracking the closet door open for a few hours at a gay bar was a particularly intense experience, both relieving but also awkward. Having been denied both the means and opportunity to develop an open system of courtship, those precious few hours at the gay bar were usually spent cutting to the chase, which is to say sucking and fucking without the arduous process of ritualized courtship.

Despite the constant threat of police harassment and subsequent public embarrassment, Café Lafitte had well established itself as a cruise bar by the mid 1960s. Consider this letter dated 1966:

Armed Forces Disciplinary Control Board
New Orleans Area
26 April 1966
Proprietor
Lafitte's in Exile
901 Bourbon St.
New Orleans, LA.

Dear Sir,

As President of the Armed Forces Disciplinary Control Board serving this locality, it is my duty to inform you of certain undesirable conditions reported at your establishment which adversely affect the health and welfare of personnel in the Armed Forces.

Inspection reports presented to the Board indicate that your establishment is a known hangout for persons of undesirable character.

You are advised that it has become necessary for this Board, which I represent, to initiate action to have your establishment declared off-limits and out-of-bounds to personnel of the Armed Forces.

If you so desire, you may appear in person, with or without counsel, before this Board at its next meeting at 0930 hours, 14 July 1966, at the US Coast Guard Station, Bayou St. John and Lakefront, New Orleans, Louisiana, to refute these allegations or to inform the Board of any remedial action you have taken, or contemplate, to correct the undesirable conditions.

It is requested that you inform the President of this Board if you plan to attend. Any questions relative to the foregoing may be addressed to the President, Armed Forces Disciplinary Control Board, U.S. Naval Air Station, New Orleans, Louisiana, and every effort will be made to clarify the matter for you.

Very truly yours,

W.F. Charles
Captain, U.S. Navy
President, AFDCB

To this day, the letter is on proud and permanent framed display on the wall near the front door of the bar.

The bar's reputation alarmed not only the U.S. military but also some gays. Albert told us he had heard of Lafitte's but "I was too chicken to go." We asked him if he remembered the first time he went to the bar: "Oh sure. I can give you the exact date: July 4, 1966—the day after I came out. I had spent the night with a really cute guy. The next day we went to the gay beach at Lake Pontchartrain[31] and later to Lafitte's. I've been a regular ever since then."

In the 1960s, years before the sexual revolution, and later, The Plague, Café Lafitte saw a lot of action. The pool table upstairs was an especially active locale in the bar. One old-timer, Ron, recalls that "All you had to do to get laid at Café

---

[31] Although not officially designated as such, there was a small section, about the length of a city block, of beachfront at Lake Pontchartrain frequented exclusively by gay men. It was not an area for public sex but it was a safe space for gay men to meet and socialize.

Lafitte was show up." Ron, who was quick to point out in his interview that he never "worked" the pool table (or roadside toilets for that matter), remembers one memorable weekend when he commandeered the restroom upstairs and serviced multiple men. Rumor has it that Confederate President Jefferson Davis' great-grandson used to hang out in the bar and give free blowjobs in the bathroom in the late 1960s.

Ralph, a forty-six-year veteran of Lafitte's, remembers first coming to the bar at the tender age of nineteen in 1964. (The drinking age was eighteen then). Initially, the bouncer wouldn't let him in because he looked too young. Ralph produced a driver's license but the bouncer wouldn't budge. Incensed, Ralph stormed off in search of a police officer to validate the license. After explaining his dilemma, the officer asked Ralph if he knew what kind of bar Lafitte's was. Ralph said yes and the cop shrugged his shoulders, walked him back to the bar and told the bouncer to let him in.

At first, Ralph was struck by how "classy" the bar was, especially when compared to the few gay bars he had been to in Memphis. For the next few years, Ralph would come to New Orleans from Tennessee three or four times a year until he finally moved to the Quarter. He describes Lafitte's in the late 1960s and '70s as having "a marvelous mix of people" and observes the bar's "attention to detail" is what made it distinctive. As an example, Ralph remembers with fondness the juicing-machine, which enabled bar patrons to witness firsthand their cocktails mixed with freshly squeezed juice. And the upstairs, he recalls, was re-decorated every few years.

Mardi Gras 1969 was a special one for Ralph. He had come down from Memphis with $100 (beer was sixty-five cents then). He met Billy, who had been a student at Tulane, by the eternal flame and the two fell madly in love. They moved briefly to California and eventually broke up after a year together. The experience transformed Ralph's life and helped him nudge his closet door more open than it had ever been before. Ralph remembers Billy, who was a bit older, telling him stories of meeting and drinking with Tennessee Williams, Truman Capote, and Gore Vidal at Lafitte's.

In Exile

Over the next four decades, Ralph would go on to meet many more men (he estimates at least 250 one-night stands from Lafitte's alone) and rack up quite a few stories himself. One memorable tryst occurred around 1980. Ralph had picked up his trick on the balcony but when they tried to leave, they couldn't get to the stairwell because the upstairs bar was so packed. No worries. The two climbed over the balcony and slid down a pole, all the while a frantic bartender was screaming, "You can't do that! You can't do that!" They hopped onto the trick's motorcycle, which was parked next to the pole and sped away to their ecstasy.

Another funny moment on the balcony occurred in the 1970s. Ralph was on the balcony smoking pot with a few friends when owner Tom Wood walked up to him and said, "You know that's only permitted if you share with the owner." Not knowing who Tom was, Ralph said, "Fuck the owner." An awkward silence ensued. Then laughter. Ralph still laughs about it today and says Tom never held it against him. That was a good business decision on Tom's part; Ralph concluded his interview by ruefully observing, "I could've had a better condo if it weren't for Lafitte's."

The upstairs bar at Lafitte's, especially the pool table area, has always been fertile ground for anonymous trysts and spontaneous encounters. Rip Naquin-Delain, co-owner and publisher of *Ambush* magazine, recalls going to Lafitte's in the late 1970s. It was the Friday before Mardi Gras and he was in town to attend a Mardi Gras ball. Afterward, he and some friends went to Lafitte's. As they ascended the stairs, Rip remembers being shocked at the scene. "Everyone was naked and having sex and here we were in our tuxes. We were lucky to get out with our clothes on."

A Tale of Two Queens? Jim Garrison and Clay Shaw

ONE OF THE MORE NOTABLE CHARACTERS to have frequented Lafitte's was prominent businessman Clay Shaw. Shaw of course achieved notoriety by being the only person ever tried in the John F. Kennedy assassination, and even though he was ultimately acquitted, his memory was further defamed by Oliver Stone's depiction of him in the film *JFK*. The trial and the movie have overshadowed Shaw's true legacy: that of a war hero, a civic leader, a French Quarter preservationist, and a successful playwright. Prior to the Garrison trial, Shaw, like countless other closeted gay leaders, was revered and respected. In 1965, the city of New Orleans awarded him its highest honor, the International Order of Merit. Many in New Orleans resent not only Stone's negative depiction of Shaw but also Jim Garrison's persecution of him. One man we interviewed, Louis, summed up the feelings of many when he called Garrison "a piece of shit who ruined Shaw."

One man who knew Shaw was Otis Fennel, owner of Faubourg Marigny Arts and Books—the first gay and feminist-themed bookstore in the South. When Oliver Stone was researching *JFK,* he hired Otis as consultant for the scenes that dealt with Clay Shaw. Shaw frequented Lafitte's so as part of the field research for the movie, Otis brought Stone to the bar. Stone told him it was the first gay bar he had ever been to. According to Otis, Stone disregarded most of the material he provided, and then refused to pay him for his consulting work. So there.

Garrison's pursuit of Shaw has been the source of much speculation. It's an open secret that Garrison was a closet case. One politically connected patron of Lafitte's is convinced that Garrison went after Shaw because both men were chasing the same twink. (It is generally conceded that Shaw had a fondness for "chicken"; several old-timers recalled that seeing Shaw cruising the Quarter in his convertible filled with young men was a common sight.) A local Monsignor who socialized with Shaw regularly is also implicated in this theory but our source declined to elaborate on the good Father's involvement. Another source of Garrison's persecution of Shaw may have been an incident one evening at Brennan's. The story goes that Garrison was at the famed restaurant dining with his first wife when the two got into a heated argument. At some point,

Garrison became so enraged he slapped his wife.[32] Shaw, who was seated at a table nearby, came over and told Garrison, "Jim, cut it out. You're not at Tony Bacino's." Garrison responded bitterly, threatening Shaw, "I'll get you for that."

Yet another theory about Garrison's motivation suggests the Shaw trial was an elaborate diversionary tactic to draw attention away from a brewing personal scandal that threatened to destroy Garrison. In 1969, a grand jury investigated allegations that Garrison had molested a thirteen-year-old boy at the New Orleans Athletic Club. At the urging of the Archbishop, and perhaps out of privacy concerns for the victim, the boy's family eventually dropped the charges, but the grand jury foreman, William J. Krummel, confirmed to columnist Jack Anderson the grand jury had looked into the allegations. Krummel never made a public comment about the investigation because he feared retribution by the District Attorney's office.

In 1998, Patricia Lambert published *False Witness: The Real Story of Jim Garrison's Investigation and Oliver Stone's film JFK*. In her research for the book, Lambert interviewed the victim and his family about the incident as well as others who knew Garrison. The portrait of Garrison that emerges is not at all flattering. David Chandler, a journalist and personal friend Garrison, said Garrison was "basically a pedophile" (236). And Rosemary James, one of the reporters who broke the news of Garrison's investigation of Shaw, notes Garrison, "used to slap his wife around in public all the time" (231). James Kirkwood, who won a Pulitzer Prize and a Tony Award for writing *A Chorus Line*, was a personal friend of Shaw's and also wrote a book about the trial, *American Grotesque*.

Other men we interviewed also recall seeing Garrison in various gay bars from time to time, particularly Le Round Up. It should be noted that Garrison was originally assigned to the prosecution team that tried the three Tulane students accused of murdering Fernando Rios in 1958. For reasons that have

---

[32] Some versions, notably the passage from Poppy Z. Brite's *Prime: A Novel*, have Garrison throwing a glass of wine in his wife's face.

never been clarified, Garrison was replaced with another assistant district attorney.

Shaw's trial dovetailed with the modern gay rights movement, which was just coming into its own at the time. Many gay men of the time believed that District Attorney Garrison's pursuit of Shaw was motivated by internalized homophobia. Consequently, they were reluctant to organize politically. That's not to say there wasn't any gay activism in New Orleans, but in retrospect, it's fair to say the persecution of Clay Shaw stifled the gay political activism burgeoning elsewhere in the nation as a result of Stonewall.

Drag Queens and Trannys

IN THE 1950S, a prepubescent boy sneaks into his sister's room to secretly wear her clothes. He likes it. It would be another thirty years before he fully embraced his suppressed identity. She knew when she was six what she was. "I was never attracted to boys. I didn't feel like a boy, but I dared not say anything." Her father was violent and once beat her to a pulp when she was fourteen because of a fight she had with her brother. Dad died shortly thereafter never knowing of his son's gender issue. Her mother once caught her wearing women's clothes, after which denial set in for both mother and son/daughter. At seventeen, she joined the Navy and served honorably for four years. In the 1960s, she led a double life as part-time man, part-time woman. It wasn't until her mother died in 1981 that Crystal Little began to live openly as a woman.

She recalls the invisibility of transgendered people in the early years.[33] The transgender community in New Orleans traces its origin to the Club My-O-My on the Lakefront which

---

[33] According to several women we interviewed, the first person to have a sex change operation in New Orleans was Alice Stevenson. Accounts of when the operation took place vary but it was either in the late 1960s or early 1970s.

featured drag shows in the 1940s and 1950s.[34] In the 1960s, a few bars in the Quarter offered occasional drag shows but performers had to arrive dressed as men and change into costume at the clubs. Likewise, said performers had to change out of costume before leaving the bars. Cross dressing was criminal and the fear of arrest and public humiliation was very real. "Things started to get better in the late 1970s," Crystal remembers. "The only reference point was Christine Jorgensen."[35]

Now sixty-six, Crystal Little administers the GLBT Community Center in the Marigny.[36] The Center opened in 1993 and Crystal has been director since 1995. The Center offers meeting space, sponsors support groups, maintains reference lists, houses a library, hosts a book club, and provides assistance to gay youth in crisis. Crystal notes the transgendered community in New Orleans is "not really an organized group, not what it should be considering its numbers. A lot of post-ops fade away into the larger community. They feel no responsibility to help others as they were helped early on." She cites great diversity within the transgender community and she identifies herself as a lesbian.

During the drag heydays of the 1980s, many drag queens banded together in communal boarding houses. Besides establishing a support network for themselves, they also

[34] The word "transgender" is problematic because it is used to describe a variety of individuals, preferences, and behaviors. These include transsexuals, cross-dressers, androgynes, genderqueers, and drag queens. In addition, these categories may be divided into further classifications. Transgender does not necessarily refer to sexual orientation.

[35] Christine Jorgensen was the first widely known person to have sex reassignment surgery. She became somewhat famous in 1952 when the *New York Daily News* claimed she was the first person to have a "sex change." This claim was not true; doctors in Germany had pioneered sex reassignment surgery in the late 1920s and early 1930s.

[36] The LGBT Community Center is located at 2114 Decatur St., New Orleans, LA, 70016 and can be reached at 504-945-1103 by phone or at www.lgccno.net.

offered assistance and guidance to young gays (not necessarily transgendered) just arriving in town or freshly out of the closet.

Paul grew up in a small town about an hour from the city and had been frequenting the gay bars since he was sixteen. In high school, he and his "straight" friends would skip school and drive to New Orleans. Somehow, they seemed to always "accidentally" end up at the gay bars. Paul eventually moved to New Orleans and secured employment at Starlight by the Park, (now Michael's on the Park) which regularly hosted (and continues to host) drag shows. In an all too familiar pattern among new arrivals, Paul developed a nasty crystal meth addiction. Legendary bartender and entertainer Marcy Marcell took him under her wing and enlisted the aid of her colleagues to help Paul overcome his addiction. It worked. Paul laughingly notes, "I didn't go to rehab, I just moved in with a bunch of drag queens!"

In 1979, Willamena came to New Orleans at the age of eighteen not knowing a soul. Thirty-two years later he is an Elder Statesman among gay bartenders in the French Quarter. Originally from Ohio, he grew up being called a sissy and a faggot. At sixteen, he found himself working as a valet at a straight nightclub in his hometown. He got along well with his boss and coworkers and many of the club's patrons. One day he was chatting with two regulars, a lesbian couple, and commented on how attracted he was to one of his male coworkers. One of lesbians asked, "You know you're a fag, right?" Willamena thought for a second and replied, "Yeah. I guess I am." The club responded enthusiastically to his coming out, embracing him and even promoting him to host on disco night. Soon after his announcement, his friends at the club ordered a fake ID from *High Times* magazine and took him to the gay clubs in nearby Cleveland.

His father did not react so well. Will's father immediately disowned him, told him to never come home again, and changed the family phone number. Unlike his own family, New Orleans welcomed him with arms wide open. He made friends and lovers easily and began an illustrious career in the service industry, bartending at several gay bars and earning a culinary degree along the way. His first few years in New Orleans were pure joy and unlimited freedom. Like so many young gay men of the time, he was reaping the fruit of the gay liberation movement and the sexual revolution:

> New Orleans really opened my eyes. I was eighteen and from a small town when I arrived in town. I got a job at The Gumbo Shop and was staying with a friend of mine from back home who had moved here. Then I ran into a drag queen on Bourbon Street coming out of a female impersonation club who I had known back home. She told me she was staying at a rooming house run by a gay guy and that I could stay there. The whole house was nothing but drag queens and trannys. One morning I went into the bathroom and there was this naked woman with big tits shaving her legs. And between those legs was the biggest, longest dick I had ever seen. I thought to myself, 'What the fuck?' Back home I had always thought of myself as a freak, but when I got to New Orleans I realized I'm gonna be okay. I can be myself here. Years later, after I thought I had seen everything, I was bartending at the Golden Lantern one Mardi Gras when two guys came in dressed as a pair of ducks. They got on the bar, bended over, and started shooting golden eggs out of their asses. I shit you not.

Transsexuality is as old as humanity itself and has long been identified with sagacity. Teiresias, the ancient blind seer from Greek mythology, was the repository of esoteric knowledge, a fusion of the sexes embodying all their attendant wisdom and insight. Camille Paglia views Teiresias as an archetype into which modern transsexuals (certainly the ones described by Paul and Willamena, as well as Crystal) easily fit:

> Teiresias, the androgynous Greek shaman, is

> depicted as an old man with long beard and pendulous female breasts . . . Teiresias . . . represents a fullness of emotional knowledge fusing the sexes . . . I adopt the name "Teiresias" for a category of androgyne, the nurturant male or male mother. He can be found in sculptures of classical river gods, in Romantic poetry (Wordsworth and Keats), and in modern popular culture (television talk show hosts) (45-46).

Marcy Marcell agreed with this assessment.[37] She estimated the number of young people she has personally helped in the dozens. And in 1987, she founded the Gay Appreciation Awards, an annual charity fundraiser. Her experience was similar to the testimony of several other transgendered people we interviewed. This quality of benevolence among the transgendered was even noted in 2000 in a *Times-Picayune* feature article about local transsexual Bobbi D'ean Perry.[38]

Willamena, and others, note that there were a lot more drag queens and transvestites in those days. There were several female impersonation clubs on Bourbon Street and a lot of the straight strip clubs were staffed by drag queens. For a time, many in the gay community called Bourbon Street "Silicon Avenue." Drag culture in New Orleans reached its zenith in the late 1970s and early 1980s. Back then performers actually sang. Lip-syncing, so common now, was virtually unheard of in those years. "A lot of them have died off but they were wonderful," Willamena observes. "They're your fiercest protectors. It's a shame so many have passed on." Many people we interviewed wistfully remembered the transgendered no longer with us: Candy Lee, Tara, Princess Mena, T.T., Betty Buttons, Ginger

---

[37] Sadly, Marcy Marcell died in 2011 not long after our interview. Her memorial service was followed by a Jazz Funeral parade that wound its way through the French Quarter and ended up at John Paul's where a grand send off party was held.

[38] Grady, Bill. "The Girl Can't Help it, So She Helps Others." *Times-Picayune* 23 July 2000.

Snap, Connie Marcell, Miss Booby, Miss Do, Miss Fly, Charmaine Montay, Terry Annette Winston, Fury, Jackie Parrish, Bobby Lane, Willow, Marcy Marcell. . .

Gay Carnival

IN THE 1960S, gays in California, Chicago, and New York began to organize politically. During the same period, the gay community in New Orleans was much more enthusiastic about organizing socially, as exemplified in the growth of gay carnival. More than a few observers have noted that "Mardi Gras is kind of gay." Edmund White offers valuable insights on this phenomenon in his landmark book, *States of Desire*:

> Mardi Gras is largely a gay holiday and drag contests are a central part of the festivities . . . I chatted with a young man from an old Cajun family who told me that he belongs not to one of the official Krewes but to an informal circle of actors, writers and painters who give eight costume balls during the season . . . In this man's opinion, gay activism in New Orleans is social, not political. "Many prominent New Orleanians, even those who are married, are gay and they are eager to protect gays. Gay life is well integrated into the life of the city" (237-38).

The Church claims Shrove Tuesday as a religious holiday, one last chance to party before Ash Wednesday and the forty days of Lent, but Carnival's pagan roots stretch back to the time before Christ was born and New Orleans knows full well she doesn't need a reason to party, much less a sanctimonious one. No, Carnival stems from the deepest core of what New Orleans is—a Pagan/Baroque fantasy realm realized, a magical make-believe playground, a mythical place of transformation.

Carnival in New Orleans is in many ways a reincarnation of the *tableaux* of King Louis XIV's Royal Court, a court whose debauchery, according to historians Will and Ariel Durant, rivaled pagan Rome at its most depraved. Consider the names of the most popular Mardi Gras krewes: Comus (God of Revelry and Excess), Momus (God of Satire), Bacchus (God of Wine), Proteus (God of the Sea and Mutability), Orpheus (God of Poets and Musicians), Endymion (God of Shepherds and Hunters), and Rex (the King of Carnival). These krewes are essentially private social clubs and it is they who annually host elaborate Carnival Balls and produce the parades for which Mardi Gras is so well known. The oldest is The Mistick Krewe of Comus, founded in 1856. The name derives from Milton's *masque*, "Comus." All the folkloric value of Mardi Gras is lost on those who view it as merely a massive drunken street orgy. S. Frederick Starr argues correctly the vulgarity of Mardi Gras is superficial, that in substance, Mardi Gras is "a poetic festival steeped in the exquisite high art of allegory" (41).

Consider the highly ritualized hallmarks of "official" Mardi Gras: by noon, Rex, King of Carnival, has arrived at Gallier Hall. The parade stops so the mayor can toast Rex. After a short speech in which the mayor decrees that merriment and revelry shall rule the day, he lifts a glass of champagne and declares, "Hail Rex!" The massive crowd follows suit, each person raising his or her drink simultaneously screaming, "Hail, Rex!" as Rex waves his scepter over the crowd and commands his subjects to have fun. At 11:30 p.m. the Rex Carnival Ball comes to a halt as Rex, his Queen, and the rest of his Royal Court make their way to pay their respects to Comus and his court at the Comus Carnival Ball. This meeting of the courts is the ritual highlight of the Carnival Season. The courts meet, toasts are made, and the band strikes up "If Ever I Cease to Love," which heralds the end of Carnival. At 12:00 a.m. Ash Wednesday is welcomed by seven policemen on horseback in wedge formation beginning the ritual sweep of Bourbon Street. Starting at Canal and followed by a small army of state troopers, they make their way down the street. The leader, armed with a bullhorn, bellows to the boozing hordes, "Mardi Gras is now over. It is Ash Wednesday. Ashes are now available at St. Louis Cathedral."

Much like New Orleans herself, Mardi Gras is a wonderfully

complex cultural phenomenon, replete with layers and layers of meaning and symbolism. It is revelry, pageantry and fantasy; who better to embody it than the gay community?

Drag performances have been associated with Mardi Gras in New Orleans since the early years of the city's existence. The earliest written reference to Mardi Gras dates back to 1729. In that year, Marc Antoine Caillot, a bureaucrat working for the Louisiana office of the Company of the Indies, wrote in his journal:[39]

> The next day, which was Lundi Gras, I went to the office where I found my companions who were bored to death. I proposed to them that we mask and go to Bayou St. John . . . As for myself, I was dressed as a shepherdess, all in white. I had a corset of white bazin, a muslin, skirt, a large pannier. . . I had some beauty marks too. I had my husband, who was the Marquis of Carnival, he had a suit trimmed with gold braid on all the seams . . . What made it hard for people to recognize me was that along with having shaved very closely that evening I had a number of beauty marks on my face and even on my breasts, which I had plumped up . . . I was the one out of all my band who was dressed up the most coquettishly . . . unless you looked at me very closely, you could not tell that I was a boy (Boyer 48-49).

Modern Mardi Gras in New Orleans dates to 1856 when a group of businessmen formed the Mistick Krewe of Comus; other krewes quickly followed, some long since passed away,

---

[39] The Caillot Manuscript describes Caillot's time in Louisiana from 1729-1731 and is housed in the Williams Research Center of the Historic New Orleans Collection. The excerpt quoted above is from an article written about the manuscript by Lori Boyer, which was published in Arthur Hardy's 2011 *Mardi Gras Guide*.

Part Two - The 1960s: The Closet Door CInches Open

others still a vibrant part of the annual celebration. Gay Carnival began in 1958 when Doug Jones and a group of his friends formed the Krewe of Yuga (KY) to spoof the mainstream krewes. The first four KY "balls" were held in private homes until the growth of the krewe and its balls' popularity necessitated a larger meeting space. One of the members taught at a school in Metairie and suggested they use the school cafeteria as the location of their fifth *bal masque*. On the night of the ball, neighbors became somewhat alarmed when they noticed dozens of gay men, many in drag, streaming into the school. The Jefferson Parish Sheriff's office was notified and just as the ball got underway, the police arrived and raided the event.

Fearing arrest and the subsequent public outing that accompanied such raids, several men ran out of the building and hid in the woods behind the school. Of the mayhem, gay carnival historian Albert Cary writes: "One story has the Queen hiding in these bushes as the troopers came through with their flashlights. Sparkling in the high beams of light, his rhinestone tiara gave him away" (para.16)[40]. After the raid, Miss Dixie hired an attorney for those arrested and paid many of the jailed men's bail. The next day's paper published the names of nearly 100 men arrested in the raid. The Krewe folded as a result of the ensuing scandal.

One of the names in the paper was Carlos Rodriguez, the first Queen of Petronius. Petronius was founded in 1961 and held its first ball in 1962. Two founding members of Petronius—Bill Wooley and Elmo Avet—had also been at the ill-fated Yuga Ball but managed to elude the police. Under their leadership, Petronius obtained a state charter and became an incorporated Carnival Krewe. Amon Ra was formed in 1966 by former Petronius members and in 1970, Jamie Greenleaf founded Olympus. Hoyle A. Byrd, Jr., who reigned as the 30th Queen of Petronius, 35th King of Petronius, and the 5th Queen of Satyricon, remembers a carnival highlight from 1969:

[40] http://www.glbtq.com/social-sciences/new_orleans_mgk.2.html

Our Krewe Captain had a beautiful apartment at the corner of St. Peter and Royal. In those days the parades still rolled through the Quarter down Royal Street. So there we were on the balcony in our elaborate costumes, part of which were hanging over the balcony, when Rex noticed us. He stopped his parade and then toasted us. That was special.

By the early 1970s, meeting space became an issue for the growing number of gay krewes.[41] Many locations were already reserved for the main-line non-gay krewes. Other locations could no longer accommodate the crowds gay balls were attracting or chose to turn a cold shoulder to them in light of the increasing visibility of the national gay rights movement. A few krewes held their balls in black union labor halls. The civic center in neighboring Chalmette became home to several krewes, which is odd since one doesn't normally associate St. Bernard Parish with tolerance and diversity.

In 1976, a disgruntled Bill Wooley broke away from Petronius and founded Celestial Knights. At its first ball, Celestial Knights tried to outshine Petronius. But Petronius, the *grande dame* of gay Carnival, would not be upstaged. In an article celebrating Petronius' 50th anniversary, Howard Smith writes:

> But the Queen of Petronius would not be outshone by her children. In her "Fantasie de la Mer" ball, the queen's costume at the end of the ball revealed her in a gloriously sequined octopus gown with tentacles spreading out to cover the entire stage. She had, for the moment, retained her luster (96-97).

---

[41] A list of gay Carnival Krewes and their founding dates are provided in Appendix B at the end of the book.

Part Two - The 1960s: The Closet Door CInches Open

Wooley was not the first, nor the last, member of a krewe to grow dissatisfied and break away to form another krewe. In 2000, longtime Petronius Captain Mickey Gil and sixteen others left to form the Mistick Krewe of Satyricon. Gil had joined Petronius in 1985, just as many krewes folded because their ranks had been decimated by the AIDS epidemic. Many credit Gill with reviving Petronius, and by extension, gay carnival, in that dark period. When he died in 2010, an article in the *Times-Picayune* honored his legacy.[42]

As of this writing, there are five active gay carnival krewes: Amon-Ra, Armeinius, Lords of Leather, Petronius, and Satyricon. In addition to the gay krewes, another immensely popular feature of gay Mardi Gras is the Bourbon Street Awards. In 1964, the owner of The Clover Grill (Arthur "Mr. Jake" Jacobs) wanted to drum up business for his diner and inaugurated a Mardi Gras costume contest. In the early years, the contest was held at the corner of Bourbon and Dumaine. From 1974 to 1985, Café Lafitte in Exile sponsored the event. In more recent years, the contest is held at the corner of Bourbon and St. Ann. Favored by drag queens and characterized by elaborate costumes, the contest draws the annual attention of the international media.[43]

Local independent filmmaker Tim Wolff has chronicled the history of gay Mardi Gras in a documentary entitled *The Sons of Tennessee Williams*, which premiered on New Orleans public broadcasting station WYES in 2011. In the film, Wolff argues the gay krewes constituted a form of gay political activism. This claim requires some qualification. The gay krewes were essentially social in nature and were not formed to further a political agenda like, say, the Human Rights Campaign or the Forum for Equality later would. Nevertheless,

---

[42] Pope, John. "Mickey Gill, Captain of Two Gay Carnival Krewes, Dies at 73." *Times-Picayune* 3 Mar. 2010.

[43] The preceding historical account is reconstructed from Smith's article, "Golden Celebration." For more detailed information on the history of specific krewes, we suggest going to krewe Web sites.

many members of the krewes were prominent members of straight New Orleans society and business circles. And some of these men did engage in activism (those who organized the Anita Bryant protests, for example, were members of gay krewes), but did not do so under the auspices of their krewe names. Also, it is important to remember that in the 1960s, gay men were routinely denied the right to free assembly (except perhaps at bars, but even that was a dicey situation given the alarming frequency and terrible consequences of police raids). The Krewe of Petronius obtaining a state charter was, therefore, a political act but not in the traditional sense of gay activism as we think of the term today.

Part Three
The 1970s: Some Damn Fool Kicks the Closet Door Wide Open

THE 1970S WERE GAY NEW ORLEANS CULTURE'S REBELLIOUS ADOLESCENCE—a time of high drama and agonizing heartache coupled with unprecedented freedom and demands for more. It was a decade of change and Café Lafitte in Exile rolled with those changes, and in many ways epitomized them. In this section we survey how and why the gay community began to assert its newfound identity as well as the ramifications of that assertion.

Tom Wood Makes a Name for Himself

THE LOOK OF CAFÉ LAFITTE remained unchanged for nearly twenty years until it underwent a major facelift in 1972. A few years earlier in 1969, Laisder Mendoza, the twenty-five-year-old son of a foreign diplomat had a heated argument with his lover in the bar and was asked by the staff to leave. Enraged, Mendoza stormed out the bar, got into his pickup truck, which was parked across the street, and drove it through the front door of the bar.[44] Three patrons were slightly injured and two were taken to Charity Hospital while the third fled the scene before the police arrived, presumably for fear of being outed. Twenty feet of the Bourbon Street façade was ripped away. Albert, a regular who lived a block away, remembers the day after incident: "The crash occurred on a Friday, but the next night was business as usual, minus the wall, of course." With the insurance money, Tom Hopkins, who now owned the bar, covered the wood structure with stucco and added the balcony with the assistance of gay architect Leon Impastato. He also converted the second floor apartment into a restaurant called The Streetcar. The Streetcar didn't last long but several remember "the food was pretty good."

In those days, the ceiling was covered with business cards and the walls of the bar were always covered with paintings from local artists. Eventually all these pieces sold with the exception of one—the one of a woman baring her breast. This painting became a fixture of the bar and came to be known by regulars as "Mother." In 1975, when Hopkins sold the bar, he refused to part with the work and had a copy of it made. It still hangs in the bar today.

In 1974, popular manager and bartender Jerry Menefee "stole" all the bartenders from Lafitte's and opened a bar of his own one block down the street called The Caverns, which later became The Bourbon Pub. At the time, it was rumored that

---

[44] "Exiled Patron Rams Pickup into Bar Door." *Times-Picayune* 3 May 1969.

Menefee opened his new bar with liquor he had stolen from the office at Lafitte's. Some of the men we interviewed refute this rumor by describing Menefee as generous and warm-hearted. These men point out that Menefee came from a wealthy family (his father was Huey Long's chief supporter in Monroe, a small city in Northeastern Louisiana). Just as many people we interviewed had no trouble whatsoever believing the rumor. Whatever the case may have been, business began to suffer at Lafitte's and the bar began to fall out of popularity.

Then along came Tom Wood. There are numerous stories of how Wood came to own the bar. Some are plausible, some are ridiculous, all are nebulous. The most outrageous theory is that he murdered his lover who had recently purchased the business and thus inherited the bar. Another wild explanation is that Wood's lover, Ben Brown, bought the bar but put it in Wood's name because Ben was a convicted felon and thereby prohibited by law from owning a drinking establishment. Some have embellished this version to have Ben's wife, who was supposedly in the dark about the bar and her husband's sexuality, going ballistic when she learned of the bar. A few even claim she came armed into the bar and began shooting. One man swears the dents in the ceiling are from the ricocheting bullets. These accounts are undoubtedly the result of years of fanciful storytelling and re-telling.

What we do know for certain is that one day in 1975, Brown and Wood came into the bar and saw Hopkins and a few others playing dice near where the DJ booth now is. Ben said, "Tom, I want to talk to you about buying the bar." Hopkins and Brown then went upstairs to discuss the matter. Hopkins agreed to sell.

By 1978, the bar was fully under Wood's ownership. The specific details and circumstances of the transaction remain nebulous. In an effort to revitalize the business, Wood removed the kitchen from upstairs and converted the restaurant to a bar called The Corral, which had a Western motif. In 1986, Wood initiated major renovations to the bar. The burlap was replaced with mahogany, which is still in use today. The bar did not close during the renovation. By this time, the bar looked much as it does today.

Wood eventually persuaded the owner of the building to sell and, in 1994, Wood purchased the building, thus ensuring Lafitte's would have a permanent home.[45] After the purchase, a huge party was thrown to celebrate and Wood burned the old lease in the eternal flame. The ashes are kept in a twenty-ounce beer go-cup in the bar's office. Café Lafitte in Exile was home for good.

In addition to saving Café Lafitte's, Wood also opened and/or saved a number of other gay bars in the French Quarter. In 1979, he opened an upscale bar with a western motif called The Great American Refuge on the corner of Royal and Ursuline. In 1984, Wood acquired The Clover Grill and opened the notorious Rawhide, which had previously been Play it Again Sam and a black gay bar. In 1988, he sold the Refuge to Jerry Menefee and opened Good Friends, previously The Louisiana Purchase. The Mystic Krewe of Barkus was born at Good Friends and remains one of the most popular Carnival parades. And in 1992, Wood opened Poppy's on St. Peter, which was essentially The Clover Grill with beer.

Wood has become something of a legend in modern gay New Orleans and, like with all legends, his life and career are surrounded by rumor and innuendo. What we know for sure is that he is an excellent businessman and the benefactor of many local charities. Without him, gay New Orleans at the turn of the millennium would look much different than it does now.

One of the more popular charity events in gay New Orleans is the Red Party, hosted annually by Café Lafitte. In 1993 or 1994, manager Robin Malta started the event, perhaps in response to the nationally renowned White Party, a weeklong circuit party held each year in Palm Springs. Each year the Red Party raises around $4,000 for a local charity.

Also, a few years ago the employees of Wood Enterprises began a fund with voluntary payroll deductions to help employees who fall on hard times. Since its inception, The

---

[45] City of New Orleans Conveyance Records lists the seller as M.J. Falgoust, Inc.

Have a Heart Fund has dispensed $3,000 to employees for various emergency expenses. Café Lafitte also participates in other community charity events such as the annual Mascara Race, a race in which participants stop at several bars to do a shot and put on an article of women's clothing.

Homophobia and the Seeds of Gay Liberation

WHEN WOOD TOOK OWNERSHIP of the bar, public attitudes concerning homosexuality in New Orleans remained stubbornly homophobic. These prejudices were reflected by the relentless efforts of police to suppress any visibility of homosexuality. Seventy men were arrested in City Park and Audubon Park during a one month period in the summer of 1976 on charges of obscenity or crimes against nature. The news coverage of these arrests reinforced the public perception of gay men as pedophiles.[46] District Attorney Harry Connick, Sr., made headlines in 1977 when he announced "the net is closing in" on sixteen men suspected of operating a "homosexual ring" out of a local Boy Scout troop.[47]

Despite the budding gay liberation movement that was gaining momentum on both coasts, gay men and women in New Orleans still feared being outed. Paul, a regular at Lafitte's for over forty years, recalls the fear of police the first time he went to the bar in the early 1970s. At that time police raids were still common and whenever a stranger entered the bar, everyone tensed up and usually fell silent. A friendly pat on the back was sufficient grounds for arrest. No one knew Paul at the time so Jerry Menefee, the bartender, asked him if he was a vice cop.

"No," Paul replied.

"Then why are you here?"

---

[46] Ussery, Bob. "Police Crackdown on Gays in Park is 'Due to Calls'." *Times-Picayune* 17 Aug. 1976.

[47] Anderson, Ed. "Additional Gay Youth Ring Charges Hinted." *Times-Picayune* 3 Nov. 1977.

"This is a gay bar, right?

"Maybe."

"Well, I'm here to get laid."

Jerry then grabbed a handful of napkins, tossed them in the air and announced loudly, "It's okay boys. He's one of us."

Paul went on to get laid several times that night. Paul lived in Houma, an hour and half away from New Orleans, but would drive in on the weekends. On one of these trips, Paul met his lover upstairs at The Bourbon Pub. They have been together thirty years.

In addition to police harassment, there was also plenty of freelance homophobia in the 1970s. Paul recalls a couple of "rednecks" were walking down Bourbon Street when they noticed a drag queen sitting at the bar inside Lafitte's. One of them stuck his head in the door and yelled, "Faggots!" Enraged, the drag queen proceeded to "kick their asses," according to Paul. After the drubbing, she stuck her very high heels on two of the redneck's throats and proudly proclaimed, "You just got your ass whooped by a faggot!"

John Meyers, local doctor who was also one of the first bartenders at The Bourbon Pub, recalls that each time he and his friends left Café Lafitte, they would look up and down Bourbon and Dumaine Streets to check not only for police but also for anyone who might recognize them.

Sometimes, police raided bars at the request of concerned citizens. One retired police officer we interviewed (a straight man who wishes to remain anonymous) remembers an incident from the early 1970s. A man informed the police that his sixteen-year-old son had run away from home and that he had tracked him to New Orleans. The father had located his son and followed him to TT's West, a gay bar on North Rampart and asked the police to retrieve him. As the police entered the bar and proceeded upstairs, they were puzzled by two large cans of Crisco at the top of the stairs. Then they beheld a sight they had surely never imagined before. There, on the pool table, the young lad was lying on his back, legs high in the air, next to another teenager (both *au naturel*) while a throng of eager patrons stood in line, dollops of Crisco in hand.

Frustration with police persecution had sparked Stonewall, widely regarded to be the birth of the modern gay rights movement. The reaction to Stonewall and the movement it engendered is impossible to separate from the *milieu* in which it occurred: the sexual revolution, the civil-rights movement, women's liberation, protests against the Vietnam War, the destabilization of white Christian hegemony. Every group of people who had been discriminated against and oppressed were rising out of their apathy and agitating for their rights, and gay folk were no exception. In New Orleans, however, the gay community was slow to organize politically and remained generally lackadaisical in demanding equality.

It was at this time that a few brave politicians began to view the gay community as a potential voting block. Longtime District Attorney Harry Connick, Sr., was the first candidate to court the gay vote in his first unsuccessful run for the office in 1969.[48] Meeting with several members of the gay community, Connick promised to end the longstanding practice of police raids of gay bars. At the meeting, which was mostly a question-and-answer session, a notoriously outspoken drag queen named Jo Jo Landry dared to ask the question that was on everyone's mind: "Let's cut the crap. What we really want to know is; are we going to go to jail if we get caught sucking dick in the bars?"[49]

In 1981, Mayor Ernest "Dutch" Morial established a Public Education Task Force to look into problems in the gay community. Gay political activists from that era agree Morial was the first mayor who demonstrated any support for the gay community and the first mayor to meet with the community. Attorney Jack Sullivan recalls the meeting. "Dutch gave a very supportive speech and the one line I'll always remember is him saying, 'As long as I'm mayor, no one will ever be discriminated

---

[48] Connick eventually won the office in 1973, succeeding Jim Garrison and serving for thirty years.

[49] Connick answered yes, noting that public sex acts, regardless of who committed them, was still illegal.

against because of his sexual *'affectation.'*"

During Mayor Morial's tenure in the 1980s, a significant change occurred within the police department. The Mayor's Advisory Commission began conducting sensitivity training at the police academy. This training essentially consisted of gay men and women recounting for cadets their own experiences as gay citizens, including personal accounts of harassment. Those who told their stories agree the training was an overall positive step in the right direction yet they all concede that reaction among the recruits was decidedly mixed.

The times were changing and public attitudes were beginning to shift, but throughout the 1970s, the city's legacy of homophobia was still fresh and very powerful in the gay community. Many gay men in New Orleans at the time believed that District Attorney Garrison's pursuit of Clay Shaw was motivated by internalized homophobia. Consequently, they were reluctant to organize politically. That's not to say there wasn't any gay activism in New Orleans but in retrospect, it's fair to say the persecution of Clay Shaw stifled local gay political activism. Nonetheless, there were a few noble attempts at political organizing.

The Gay Liberation Front of New Orleans was founded in 1970. Although the group fell apart by mid-1971, in that brief span it had produced the first gay public action, a demonstration at City Hall protesting police harassment consisting of about seventy-five protesters. The march on City Hall received moderate coverage in the press. *The Times Picayune* even printed the marcher's demands:

1. An immediate end of all hostility, brutality, entrapment and harassment by the New Orleans Police of gay men and women and of their places of gathering.
2. Formation of a Governor's Panel empowered to conduct a complete and thorough investigation of the police methods and actions against gay people. On this panel shall sit one gay man and one gay woman.

3. The immediate suspension from duty of Police Superintendent Clarence Giarusso and Vice Squad head Souler, until the Governor's Panel has completed its investigation. Should the panel find against these men, they shall be terminated immediately.[50]

The demands were disregarded but did not go unnoticed. Straight New Orleans was shocked not only at the visibility of gay people but also, perhaps more so, at the alarming fact they were demanding things. While the Gay Liberation Front disturbed many straight people, it also gave hope to many gays who were still in the closet. One man we interviewed told us it had never occurred to him to live openly gay until the GLF's march on City Hall.

The GLF also published the first gay-identified publication; a newsletter entitled *Sunflower*. The first edition featured testimonials from several men, one of whom was straight, who were harassed, beaten, and arrested while in or near Cabrini Park,[51] which was, apparently, quite the cruising ground. The GLF also presented the first Stonewall commemoration, a June 1971 "Gay-In" in City Park. Out of the organizing efforts of the Gay Liberation Front, individuals soon founded a Metropolitan Community Church congregation, a Daughters of Bilitis chapter, and a gay student organization at Tulane University.

Dovetailing with the emerging women's liberation movement, lesbians began to organize and several women's groups were formed, including a lesbian music festival. Many lesbians became involved with NOW (the National Organization for Women) in an effort to get the ERA (Equal Rights Amendment) passed. A Lesbian Task Force was formed and even traveled around the state on educational tours. The primary lesbian bars of this period were Charlene's on Elysian Fields and Alice Brady's bar Mr. D's Hideaway on Dauphine.

---

[50] "Gay Liberation Group Marches." *Times-Picayune* 24 Jan. 1971.

[51] Now commonly known as The Dog Park.

Clay Latimer, an early lesbian activist who was arrested in a raid at Charlene's, remembers bringing a typewriter and index cards to Charlene's to solicit political messages from patrons. "Charlene's didn't mind political activity, but that sort of thing was forbidden at Alice Brady's bars."

The Fire

ON JUNE 24, 1973, a Sunday evening, an unruly hustler, Rodger Dale Nunez, was physically thrown out of The Upstairs Lounge bar for badgering and fighting with a regular customer, Mike Scarborough. Scarborough was in the bathroom when Nunez, who was in the next stall, started harassing him through the glory hole. Scarborough complained to the bartender. As Nunez was being escorted out the bar, he threatened to "burn you all out." About thirty minutes later, a fire broke out on the stairwell. As the fire spread, panic ensued. Bartender Buddy Rasmussen led about twenty people through a rear fire exit which was not clearly marked. Many dashed for the window but the window had burglar bars. A few, including a man named Rusty, were skinny enough to squeeze through but the others were doomed.[52]

Katherine Kirsch was on her way to buy cigarettes around 7:45 p.m. when she smelled smoke at the corner of Iberville and Chartres. She opened the stairwell, saw the flames and immediately ran to The Midship Bar next door to call the police. Fire trucks arrived about two minutes later. They were met by a grizzly, horrific scene. A few who had jumped lay charred and dead on the sidewalk. The lifeless body of Bill Larson, pastor of the local Metropolitan Community Church, was wedged in the window, his face and right arm protruding stiffly over the street. Buddy Rasmussen saw his boyfriend Adam Fontenot knocked off his feet with a blast from a fire

---

[52] The Williams Research Center of the Historic New Orleans Collection has a wealth of archival material on the fire including a copy of the police report and a fascinating ninety-six page unpublished document compiled by Johnny Townsend which offers biographical sketches of the victims.

hose while he flayed around on fire. George Mitchell had escaped the fire but ran back into to rescue his boyfriend, Louis Broussard; their bodies were found intertwined, thereby occupying in death a position they often occupied in life. Many of the dead were burned beyond recognition but were ultimately identified through the dental records of local dentist Perry Waters, who also perished in the fire.[53]

Thirty men and two women died that night.[54] Nunez committed suicide the following year. According to drag queen Marcy Marcel and several others, Nunez killed himself because he was so full of remorse. Although Marcy was a regular at The Upstairs Lounge on Sunday nights at the time, she stayed at home that night to watch a Bette Davis movie (*Jezebel*). Everyone we interviewed who was in New Orleans at the time remembered where they were the night of the fire. Albert Carey, for example, was at The Saenger Theatre watching *Cabaret*. "My mom had seen the news report and was so worried about me because she kept calling me, but I wasn't home. She thought I might have been at the bar."

Initial media reports and the police response to the fire were less than sympathetic. Some family members of the deceased refused to claim the ashes of their "loved" ones. Radio commentators joked the remains should be buried in fruit jars. Church after church refused the use of their facilities for a memorial service. Father Bill Richardson of St. George's Episcopal Church, however, believed the dead, despite their lifestyles, should have a service and graciously allowed, over the protest of many parishioners, the use of St. George's sanctuary. Marcy Marcel, who was at the service, echoed the feelings of others when she recalled being relieved to see her friends alive if not altogether well, at the service. After the

---

[53] This reconstruction of events is adapted from Skylar Fein's *Remember the Upstairs Lounge*, self published as a companion to an exhibit of Fein's artwork commemorating the fire. For more information on the exhibit, visit Skylarfein.com

[54] The names of the deceased are listed in Appendix D at the end of this book.

service, Reverend Perry, who officiated, pointed out a rear entrance for those who wished to avoid the television cameras which waited outside the main entrance. No one took his offer.

The Upstairs arson attracted gay activists from all over the country to New Orleans, most notably The Reverend Troy Perry, founder of the Metropolitan Community Church. Perry and others chastised the gay community of New Orleans for its apathetic attitude and general lethargy regarding the gay liberation movement so much in vogue in other American cities at the time. Local bar owners and prominent gay men responded by calling Perry and the other activists "carpetbaggers" and "outside agitators." John Meyers, a retired obstetrician who worked his way through medical school by bartending at several gay bars, recalls meeting Perry at Café Lafitte and telling him firmly, "Leave us alone." Looking back thirty-eight years later, Meyers admits, "Perry was right." The carpetbaggers, and straight locals, assumed then, and still believe today, the fire was an act of hate motivated by homophobia. They couldn't be more wrong.

The fire motivated a handful of activists to form the Gay People's Coalition (GPC). The GPC launched another publication, *Causeway*, and established the Gay Crisis Phone Line. *Causeway* was edited anonymously by a Tulane student named Bill Rushton, who also edited *The Vieux Carré Courier*. An editorial from the January 1974 edition of *Causeway* declared, "There are enough gay men and women in N.O. who are able to do anything they wish—be it swinging an election or electing a gay city councilman" (Sears 273). This clarion call, while certainly true, fell on deaf ears. As the embers of the fire cooled, so did the ire of the gay community. In what was to become the dominant pattern of gay activism in New Orleans, the GPC, and *Causeway*, eventually faded away.

In 2008, The Upstairs Lounge tragedy was memorialized with an art exhibit by Skylar Fein at the Contemporary Arts Center as part of the first annual Prospect 1, a city-wide collection of art exhibits. It was restaged in 2010 in New York by No Longer Empty. The exhibit received glowing reviews from art critics, but some gay men had not-so-favorable reactions. One man angrily told the artist, "Of all the things in our community, why pick this?" And one foundation, to which Fein appealed for funding the project, declined his request not with a standard rejection form letter but rather with a hand written note from the foundation's director, a man who lived in New Orleans at the time of the fire. This man wrote, "Have a little bit of the pain of what it was like to be gay then." The horror of the fire and the anguish it engendered still burns hot.

A Spurt of Activism

THE UPSTAIRS LOUNGE FIRE was a seminal moment in the history of gay New Orleans, the significance of which was even noticed by the arch-conservative *Times-Picayune*. A month and a half after the fire, the paper published a week-long series of six articles, all written by Joan Treadway, concerning homosexuality, the first of which was titled, "Gay Community Surfaces in Tragedy of N.O. Fire."[55] The tone of the article is surprisingly objective and Treadway even quotes local gay activists who succinctly summarized the multitude of dilemmas facing gay New Orleanians: police harassment, job and housing discrimination, and general societal alienation.

The second article in the series, "Independent Route Taken for Personal Objectives,"[56] offered various gay persons' views of how the newly created New Orleans Gay People's Coalition would affect their lives as gay New Orleanians. The third article, "Homosexuals Disagree on Behavior's Sickness,"[57] explored the debate within the psychiatric community over whether homosexuality should be removed from the American

---

[55] Treadway, Joan. "Gay Community Surfaces in Tragedy of N.O. Fire." *Times-Picayune* 11 Sept. 1973.

[56] Ibid. "Independent Route Taken for Personal Objectives." *Times-Picayune* 12 Sept. 1973.

[57] Ibid. "Homosexuals Disagree on Behavior's 'Sickness'." *Times-Picayune* 13 Sept. 1973.

Psychiatric Association's list of mental disorders. A year later, in 1974, the APA finally voted to no longer consider homosexuality an illness. The fourth article, "Psychiatric and Clerical Views—a Wide Spectrum," elaborated on the debate within psychiatric circles and included the views of a Baptist pastor, which were predictably ludicrous—"if preachers condone homosexuality, they're anti-Christs, enemies to God in Clerical garb."[58] The next article, "It's Not Illegal to BE Gay—Certain Acts are Criminal,"[59] enumerated the legal prohibitions against gay sex (a $2,000 fine and five years in prison) and detailed how law enforcement attitudes were in the process of changing. The final article, "'50s 'Climate of Hostility' to Gays Gone—What Now?"[60] surveyed how attitudes had shifted from hostility to begrudging tolerance over the previous decades. As one might expect the series elicited a wide variety of responses, both positive and negative, from readers.

This fair and balanced treatment represented a colossal paradigm shift in the print media's treatment of gay issues. Two years later, Gail Shister, reporter for *The New Orleans States-Item*, would become the nation's first openly gay lesbian working for a major daily newspaper.

In addition to provoking interest in the print media, the fire also inspired some political activism. Former Baptist minister Mike Stark formed the Gay Services Center, located on Burgundy in the Marigny, in 1974. Initially the group enjoyed a flurry of activity, including the publication of a newsletter, *The Closet Door*. But the group's promise was never fulfilled. In a familiar pattern, the newsletter and the group were soon moribund.

One short-lived yet somewhat successful attempt at organizing was the formation of the Gertrude Stein Society in

---

[58] Ibid. "Psychiatric and Clerical Views—a Wide Spectrum." *Times-Picayune* 14 Sept. 1973.

[59] Ibid. "It's Not Illegal to BE Gay—Certain Acts are Criminal." *Times-Picayune* 15 Sept. 1973.

[60] Ibid. *Times-Picayune* 16 Sept. 1973.

1975. Founded by Bill Rushton and his boyfriend Alan Robinson, both of whom were regulars at Café Lafitte, the GSS succeeded in assembling a mailing list, publishing a newsletter (*Gertrude's Notes*), and hosting a variety of social and political events, the most amazing of which was the first gay TV talk show: *Gertrude Stein Presents*. In one episode, Rushton interviewed Christine Jorgensen, whose sex change in 1951 had shocked the world. Her appearance galvanized the slumbering political consciousness of the local gay community and soon businesses and politicians began to court the gay community. Gay activism in New Orleans had finally produced some results, meager for sure, but results nonetheless. This momentum may have evaporated, but in a gift of great timing, the nation's leading homophobe announced she was coming to New Orleans.

In 1977, anti-gay crusader and Florida orange juice spokesperson Anita Bryant arrived in New Orleans to perform in concert. It was the homophobic singer's first public appearance after her successful campaign to overturn a gay rights ordinance in Miami. All the gay bars in New Orleans immediately stopped serving Florida orange juice and the Gertrude Stein Society announced a protest rally and hoped that a hundred people would venture out of their closets and into the bright light of day. The organizers were astonished at the turnout. Several thousand demonstrators rallied in Jackson Square and marched through the French Quarter to the Municipal Auditorium where Bryant was performing. In his landmark book on Southern gayness, *Rebels, Rubyfruit, and Rhinestones,* James Sears describes the protest as the defining moment of gay activism in New Orleans:

> The crowd held hands and sang "We Shall Overcome." Looking up to the threatening sky, Leonard Matlovich shouted, "Lord, don't rain on our parade." Cadenced cheers rippled across the crowd. As the sun broke through the clouds, Frank Kameny proclaimed: "We will not continue to live in closets."

> Demonstrators began their march through the Quarter walking down St. Ann Street, chanting "Out of the Closets and into the Streets." Supporters on wrought iron balconies wrapped with banners cheered. The march extended four blocks from sidewalk to sidewalk as it turned on Bourbon and headed to Dumaine, picking up marchers along the way. Marking one of the largest civil rights demonstrations in the city's history, thousands of protesters arrived at the North Rampart Street Municipal Auditorium entrance. The protesters were elated: "the reaction within the ranks was explosive, euphoric, and pure; the silence of the past is ended" (276).

Bryant's announcement to come to New Orleans also spurred a short-term coalition of gay and gay-friendly groups to form HERE (Human Equal Rights for Everyone). The concert did go on and enjoyed moderate success but HERE was successful in pressuring local radio stations to not air Bryant's performance.

Also in 1977, boyfriends Roy Letson and Gary Martin founded *Impact*, a gay-themed newspaper.[61] A year later author Tom Horner opened the Faubourg Marigny Bookstore, the first gay/feminist bookstore in the South. In the same year, the Pink Triangle Alliance commemorated the first anniversary of the Bryant protest with another June rally in Jackson Square. This effort led to Gayfest.

Gayfest produced its first Pride celebration in 1978. In the following few years the emerging gay community included a wide range of social, service, religious, and sports organizations: the Louisiana Gay Political Action Caucus was founded in 1980, a state Gay Conference was held in 1981, the New Orleans Gay Men's Chorus was founded in 1982, the local chapter of PFLAG was founded in 1982, and in 1983 the

---

[61] Back-issues of *Impact* are available at the main branch of the New Orleans Public Library and in the archives of the New Orleans GLTB Center.

NO/AIDS Task Force consolidated health efforts initiated by other groups.

New Orleans PFLAG co-founder Niki Kearby says PFLAG grew out of her dissatisfaction with her own church's intolerance of homosexuality; specifically, a friend who worked in the administrative offices of the church who was fired when she admitted to being gay. Kearby, who grew up a devout Methodist and was a member of Rayne Methodist Church on St. Charles Ave., began attending St. Mark's United Methodist Church which had a gay-friendly pastor. The earliest PFLAG meetings were held at a Catholic Community Center on Barracks Street in a very small room. About twenty people attended the first meeting, half of whom had to sit on the floor. *The Times-Picayune* initially refused to run an ad for the meeting but after some string pulling, the paper's owner acquiesced and ran the ad. Attendance increased and the meetings were eventually moved to Mercy Hospital. In 1987, the PFLAG scholarship program began with a generous donation from Rich Sacher and his partner.

Also in the early 1980s, there were several "Celebration Weekends"—conferences that included workshops, social events, and networking opportunities. Stewart Butler recalls the purpose of Celebration was "educational and inspirational." Jody Gates also notes, "Celebration meetings helped the coming out process." And Clay Latimer adds, "Celebration eventually wound down because the need for it diminished." In 1981, The Crescent City Coalition, a political activist group, was formed.

The Gay Underbelly as Artistic Inspiration

IN 1963 JOHN RECHY PUBLISHED *City of Night*, an autobiographical novel recounting his experiences working as a male prostitute in various American cities, including New Orleans. The book established Rechy as a pioneer of GLBT literature. Later, Rechy credited New Orleans as being the inspiration for the work. "*City of Night* began as a letter to a friend of mine after I had been to New Orleans. I wrote *City of*

Night because they were my experiences hustling . . ."[62] Rechy was not the first, nor would he be the last, writer to find inspiration in the underbelly of New Orleans' street life. This scene has been especially fruitful for gay writers and artists.

Perhaps the most prolific and one of the most prominent, gay artists in New Orleans is George Dureau. Known primarily for his studies of the nude male figure and black and white homoerotic photography, Dureau has had exhibits in Paris, London, New York, Los Angeles, and other cities around the United States. For subjects, Dureau looks to the classic male nude in all its chiseled perfection, but he just as often draws upon homeless youths, dwarfs, amputees, the obese, and others who do not conform to mainstream society's traditional standards of beauty. Dureau's frankness of depiction typically brings to life his subjects' beauty and dignity.

Humanities professor Claude Summers has argued that Dureau's photography influenced the legendary gay photographer Robert Mapplethorpe:

> Dureau's photographs have often been compared with those of Robert Mapplethorpe. But the influence runs not from Mapplethorpe to Dureau but from Dureau to Mapplethorpe. The photographers were friends in the early 1970s. Mapplethorpe was greatly moved by Dureau's photographs, even to the point of restaging many of Dureau's earlier compositions.
>
> For all their similarities, however, the photographs of Dureau and Mapplethorpe are quite different. Whereas Mapplethorpe exhibits his subjects as cool and objective, self-contained and remote icons, Dureau presents his as exposed and vulnerable, playful and needy, complex and entirely human individuals. The difference is foremost a matter of empathy.

---

[62] http://www.johnrechy.com/city.htm

In his photographs, as in his paintings, Dureau is not a detached observer. He conveys a deep artistic and psychological involvement with his subjects not merely as objects but also as human beings. Consequently, the photographs induce the viewer's involvement, invoking emotional as well as intellectual and aesthetic responses.

In 1999, Douglas MacCash, art critic for *The Times-Picayune*, reviewing a Dureau retrospective on display at the Contemporary Arts Center, elaborated on the relationship between Dureau and Mapplethorpe:

But in spite of their similar interest in figural photography, the two men found little common ground in their working methods. Mapplethorpe was impatient with Dureau, who spent countless hours conversing with his models, dining, drinking and strolling the French Quarter before he began a photo session. Then he cajoled his models into poses that were partially of his design, but also partially of their making. Why, Mapplethorpe wanted to know, didn't he just pay them and tell them what to do?

Dureau was taken aback by the younger man's abruptness and indifference to the people he photographed. Dureau did pay his models outright, but he also befriended them in a way Mapplethorpe could not understand. It's no surprise, then, that one of the major differences between their work is that Dureau's has a certain sense of intimacy that Mapplethorpe's lacks. Mapplethorpe's "Black Book" of 1986, a portfolio of photos of African Americans, is a tribute to Dureau's influence.[63]

---

[63] MacCash, Douglas. "Opening the Shutter." *The Times-Picayune*. 22 Oct. 1999.

The contrast MacCash paints between the two artists is characteristic of the differences between the two cities in which they grew up, New Orleans and New York respectively—New York: impersonal, all business and ever in a hurry; New Orleans: friendly, lazy and slow. This affable lethargy is often one of the first qualities of New Orleans that transplants notice when they arrive. Artist Skylar Fein describes it this way, "People here are lulled into a slow, easy life. They want to luxuriate in slow moments. In New York you brag about how busy you are; here you brag about how much time you have."

Fein is one of the more promising gay artists living and working in New Orleans today. His artistic debut was an exhibit at the Jonathan Ferrara gallery for Prospect 1 in 2008. The following year he had a solo exhibit at the New Orleans Museum of Art, and in 2010 at VOLTA NY. Fein's work has been favorably reviewed in notable publications such as *Art in America, ArtForum, The New York Times, The New Yorker*, and *The Times-Picayune*, but when he came to New Orleans in 2005, he had no artistic training whatsoever. The story of his success is a fascinating account of how New Orleans, even at its worst, is a source of artistic inspiration.

Originally from New York, Fein moved to New Orleans six weeks before Hurricane Katrina. He evacuated to Tennessee for a month and upon returning to New Orleans, realized he needed furniture. Combing through the endless piles of rubble that littered the city, he gathered enough debris to build a table and chairs. His ingenuity impressed his friends and others and soon he was meeting a demand for more furniture. This endeavor awakened his creativity, and then one day he was walking down Iberville Street when he noticed a plaque on the sidewalk commemorating The Upstairs Lounge Fire. Upon reading the plaque, Fein recalls thinking to himself, "How do I not know about this?"

"The seediness of the block" and "the handsomeness of the building" was "tantalizing" and thus ensued six months of research into the fire which culminated in his exhibit, "Remembering the Upstairs Lounge." That exhibit established

Fein as an up-and-coming artist, but it wasn't his first exhibit. Fein's premiere exhibit was at the notorious leather bar The Phoenix. Fein in his own words:

> A casual tourist to 1950s New Orleans might have missed the seedy second-floor bookstore on Rampart Street. But in the gay subculture of the time, Henkin's Adonis, with its cruisy magazine racks, private booths and tiny movie theater, was a place notorious and beloved.
>
> When the city bulldozed the area to build a park in 1971, a treasure trove of gay history was lost.
>
> But it wasn't lost forever.
>
> In 2005, gay photographer Leonard Earl Johnson was clearing out a friend's garage just outside the Quarter—the friend was elderly and no longer had the strength to do hurricane cleanup—when he made a surprising find: a dusty old sign with a picture of a cowboy.
>
> He wiped his hand across it, and as he made out the word "Henkin," he got a shiver of recognition. He looked around the garage. It was stacked with the original signs of Henkin's Adonis—three decades of them. When he showed them to me the next day, he was still shaking with excitement.
>
> I told the manager of the local leather bar about the staggering find. She suggested an art show—right there in the bar. So on Saturday night, in the back room of the second sleaziest bar in New Orleans, we hung the signs of Henkin's Adonis. Crowds of gay men came to pay homage to the lost Atlantis of sleaze, sex and self-acceptance.
>
> There's just one thing wrong with this story. I made it up.
>
> Henkin's Adonis never existed. I painted the

signs myself, lovingly sketching believable images (cowboys, farm hands) and tag lines ("Physique and body-building")—code words that gay men in the 1950s and '60s understood. I distressed the signs, sanding and rubbing them with dirt to simulate the passing of so many years.

But here's the weird part. (That was the normal part.) The men who came to the opening remembered the Adonis in every detail.

They recounted the flirtations among the magazines, the hand-jobs in the tiny theater, the time they were arrested coming out...of Henkin's Adonis. I had crafted bogus newspaper articles from the Adonis' last day (never happened), when patrons famously rioted against the cops sent to clear the building (completely false), when locals held a vigil and brought flowers as the bulldozers revved up (a fantasy), and I'd blown up the clippings and hung them on the wall, too. People remembered the coverage.

I would say that half the bar knew it was a lark, and the other half was absolutely convinced it was real and had the memories to prove it. If anyone asked me directly, I told the truth: it was my homage to the gay men of another time, whose fighting and loving made it possible for me to live openly today. But to the men who talked and talked without asking a question, I simply smiled and nodded along, a student of their sometimes unsteady eldership.

This probably says a lot about memory, its creation and fabrication. It may say a lot about gay men, or about New Orleans, which still provides the gutter for all America to lie in cheaply and conveniently. All I know for sure is what the Adonis sign says: "We never close."

Uptown Gays and Downtown Gays

ISSUES OF CLASS AND RACE is very real in New Orleans and, in some ways, typifies the contradictions that define the city. On one hand, the city is well integrated to a certain extent. On the other hand, everyone knows his place in the social order. In the nineteenth century and for most of the twentieth, race was the dominant factor in the social structure, but not race in terms of black and white; rather, the crux of the racial issue was Creole versus American. Free people of color represented a sizable demographic and even women, because of Creole legal precedents, enjoyed more liberty than their counterparts in the rest of the country (they could own property and had a limited right to vote on property issues twenty years before universal suffrage). The Americans, the business elite, settled up-river in the Garden District and along St. Charles Avenue. Creole society had already established itself in the lower Quarter and along Esplanade Avenue. Today, many descendents of the Creole elite reside in the 7th Ward. Perhaps because of the rivalry with Creole Society or perhaps because of a tendency toward exclusiveness in their nature, the Americans have formed a virtually impenetrable social circle. Louisiana political observer John Maginnis has noted:

> Pedigree counts for more in New Orleans than in any other big city in the country. The Old Guard, the descendents of the first American families to settle in the city (they were very much the New Guard to the French and Creole families living in the French Quarter in the early 1800s), have shut the door tight to social acceptance. It is said that major corporations are reluctant to base operations and officers in New Orleans because their daughters can't be presented to society and the executives, no matter how big their paycheck, can't eat at the Boston Club (116).

We previously cited Edmund White's classic book *States of*

Desire, particularly a New Orleanian he interviewed who observed, "Many prominent New Orleanians, even those who are married, are gay and they are eager to protect gays. Gay life is well integrated into the life of the city" (239). Eager to explore this "integration," White also interviewed others about their gay life in New Orleans. One young man observed:

> I grew up in the Garden District. My parents always had wild alcoholic parties. My uncle was gay and I can remember as a child going to visit him in his own sitting room during one of my parent's parties. There he'd be with his other gay friends, all aunties, and they'd be sitting there in dresses. No one raised an eyebrow. I didn't think of myself as gay. I knew many men who were married and gay, and I thought I'd be like them. It's called an "uptown marriage." You live with your wife and children uptown and you keep a boy in the Quarter. In the last century the Creoles kept mistresses in the Quarter, and more than one kept a boy—it's a very old custom. I had a fiancée. She and I had grown up together. She had given me her virginity and that was a very big deal. When I was seventeen I started sneaking off to Lafitte's. I'd take her home after dates and usually end up at the bar. One night she was drunk and suspicious and she followed me to the bar. At the bar she demanded that the bouncer let her in: "I've come to see my husband." She and I started having a knock-down drag-out when we suddenly looked up and there, coming down the stairs from the bar above, was her father! (White 240).

With regard to Uptown gays, class continues to trump gender, especially when gender is bended. The age-old Creole-American divide in New Orleans lives on in the gay community. There are a large number of professional gay men who are part of the elite business establishment (including more than a few former Rexes) who choose to remain closeted and who rarely frequent the gay bars in the Quarter, Marigny, and Bywater. In the early 1970s, many of them gathered and socialized at the New Orleans Athletic Club and Ched's on St. Charles Ave. The men's rest rooms at Maison Blanche and D.H. Holmes Department stores were also favorite cruising grounds, as were certain sections of City Park and Audubon Park. There was also an annual gathering in Pensacola at the San Carlos Hotel.

The dichotomy between Uptown and Downtown (particularly the Quarter), is perhaps best illustrated in a story Tennessee Williams recounts in his *Memoirs*. Disappointingly, Williams doesn't offer much insight into his life in New Orleans in that work, but this anecdote is telling:

> At first I lived a very reclusive life for a resident of New Orleans, that gregarious city . . . I was entertained a good deal by the elite New Orleans society which in those days resided mainly, if not entirely, on the far side of Canal Street, in what is called the Garden District.
>
> One evening I felt well enough to give my socially elite friends a party in my little apartment on Orleans Street. Probably some of the young debutantes had never before entered an apartment in the Vieux Carré unless it were in the Pontalba buildings that were on Jackson Square, the only "respectable" dwellings in the Quarter. I mean recognized as such by the Garden District mothers.
>
> My party was a curious occasion.
>
> I remember a young debutante inquiring if she could see my bedroom.
>
> "Why not? It's very nice."
>
> "He's going to show us his bedroom!" exclaimed the young lady. The whole party trooped in.

They seemed to like the bedroom . . . Then somebody turned to my apartment mate. "Now show us yours."

He probably knew that a scandal was brewing and would have wished to avoid it but I found it perfectly natural to say, "We share this room."

I thought the silence that followed my statement was not natural at all.

You see the bed was somewhere between single and double . . .

Debutantes began to whisper to their escorts, there were little secretive colloquies among them and presently they began to thank us for an unusual and delightful evening and to take their leave as though a storm were impending. . .

About half an hour after the escorted debutantes had taken to their heels and my friend and I were about to retire, there came a short nervous rap at the door. I threw on my dressing gown and opened the door upon the handsomest of the young men that had attended our party. He wore only a raincoat and immediately after the door was opened for him, he flung his coat off, rushed into the bedroom and fell sobbing drunkenly on the bed.

"At last a little truth and they couldn't take it," he kept saying, until we put him to sleep (100-01).

Williams knew the "Uptown mentality" well, having lived for a time at The Pontchartrain Hotel on the edge of the Garden District. For most of his time in New Orleans, though, Williams lived in the French Quarter, maintaining at various times, three different apartments. Lafitte's was Williams' favorite bar and he remained a regular there until his death in 1983. John Meyers recalls meeting Williams at the bar in 1975:

I was sitting at the bar and I knew who he was but

I didn't make a big deal out of it. Then he came over and introduced himself as Tom, which was his given name. We fell into conversation and he ended up taking me to lunch at Antoine's. I was in medical school at the time and thinking of going into psychiatry. He spoke of his sister's lobotomy—something I don't think he ever recovered from. He seemed more interested in drinking than eating. In fact, I ate most of his food. We had a wonderful conversation and overall it was a delightful afternoon.

The French Quarter Slasher and Other Queer Murders

IN THE EARLY 1970S, a handful of gay men met every Friday afternoon for cocktail hour at Pete's, a bar on the corner of Bourbon and St. Ann. One of those men was John Meyers. At one of the weekly gatherings, John met a fresh face, Jack—a charming young man who was new to the group. On the Saturday of Super Bowl weekend 1972, John was running errands in the Quarter when he ran into Jack at The Lemon Tree, a boutique shop on Royal. John greeted Jack but Jack said nothing. Shrugging his shoulders, John took his leave and went to the A&P. Again he sees Jack and again Jack says nothing. This happened again at a third store. Unsure what to make of Jack's strange behavior, John headed home to his apartment on Chartres Street. Jack was waiting for him outside the building and this time he spoke, "Johnny, can I come upstairs?" The two proceed upstairs and without a word, Jack unzipped John's pants, gave him a blow job, and then left quietly afterwards. John recalls, "That surprised me because I didn't think Jack found me attractive."

Twenty minutes later, John heard frantic screaming from the downstairs apartment where his ex-lover Dick Swanson lived with his boyfriend Chuck. John rushed to the apartment to find Dick lying on the floor bleeding profusely from the chest. Chuck, who had been in the shower, was standing there horrified, and at the kitchen table sat Jack, blank-faced, with a bloody knife in his hand. Chuck said, "He's killed the man I wanted to spend the rest of my life with."

John ran back upstairs and called the police and also Jim Blackman, who was a part of the Friday cocktail club. The police came and arrested Jack. John was holding Dick in his arms when he died. Jack was found to be insane and was committed to the Mental Institution in Jackson.

Later it was discovered that Jack, under the influence of some exceptionally strong hallucinogenic drugs, had brutally murdered a bartender at one of the gay bars on Iberville Street and chopped the body to pieces the day before he killed Dick. The theory is that he confessed the crime to Dick and Dick told him he had to turn himself in. Not wanting to hear that, Jack murdered Dick. John remembers Dick's parents coming in from California. "They wanted to see what it was about New Orleans that Dick loved so much. So I showed them around." John remained friends with them for years, visiting them regularly when he did his residency in San Francisco. "They never got over Dick's death."

Because of the gay aspect of the case, the crime was not reported in the media. But this grisly double murder was a mere foreshadowing of a murder spree that would demand media attention a few years later.

In the spring of 1977, a headline in *The Times-Picayune* read, "Quarterites Ask Protection from Slasher."[64] A serial killer targeting gay men was on the loose in the lower Quarter and residents were frustrated with police, the article explains. In a two month span, five men were murdered: Robert Gary, Jack Savell, Alden D. Delano, James McClure, and Ernest Pommier. Sixteen-year-old Warren Harris was eventually arrested on a tip from two African-American drag queens for the murders. During questioning, Harris, who had a transsexual roommate, spoke of his "revulsion for homosexuals."[65] Harris was convicted in three of the five

---

[64] "Quarterites Ask Protection from Slasher." *Times-Picayune* 10 April 1977.

[65] Ibid.

murders. A severe case of internalized homophobia was apparently the motive in Harris' slaying spree.

Homophobia was the motive in another high profile murder in 1993. Early one Thursday morning in November, twenty-three-year-old Joseph Balog and a friend were walking down Dauphine Street when they were attacked by four men who taunted them with gay slurs. Balog and his friend were not gay but that didn't matter to the vicious mob. Balog was stabbed in the chest, back, and hand and was found lying on the sidewalk of St. Philip Street between Dauphine and Bourbon. A Quarter resident out walking his dog found Balog bleeding to death and barely conscious. He was rushed to Charity Hospital, where he died. His friend managed to escape the bloody attack. The following night, Lin-Todd Soldani organized among the gay community and other Quarter residents a rally and candlelight march to the location of the murders.[66] Police arrested Ronald Graves for the murder but at trial the jury deadlocked.

Another serial killer targeting gay men in the French Quarter surfaced in 1984. Early in that year, five men were bludgeoned with a hammer, three of whom died. Three of the men were gay bar owners, former owners, or bartenders. The killer was never apprehended and the murders remain unsolved.

The first murder reported after Hurricane Katrina involved long-time *Impact* columnist and editor Jon Newlin. On November 14, 2005, Newlin was enjoying a quiet evening at his home in the Marigny when ex-boyfriend Cleveland Moore showed up with Joyce Rader, whom Newlin did not know. The three were casually socializing when Moore grabbed a wine bottle and savagely attacked Newlin as Rader watched with a smile on her face. The next morning, Newlin's friend Mark Baringer found him lying on the floor, severely beaten but still alive. Rader, who had a history of drug addiction and prostitution charges, was dead in the kitchen.

Moore, who had worked as a stripper at the Unisex Club on

---

[66] Grissett, Sheila. "Police: Men Stabbed by Gay Bashers." *Times-Picayune* 20 Nov. 1993.

Bourbon Street, was eventually arrested in Florida and extradited to Louisiana where he now resides at Angola State Prison. Despite his identifying Moore as his attacker, Newlin told us the police "were not that interested" in tracking down Moore. Judith Wenger, a friend of Newlin's, *was* interested and located him through an Internet search. Moore was convicted in the attack on Newlin and also in Rader's murder. Newlin, now paralyzed down his left side, has been confined to a wheelchair since the brutal beating.

Part Four
The 1980s: The Closet Door Falls Off Its Hinges

THE 1980S WAS A TIME OF RECKONING and transition for the gay community in New Orleans. Having reached young adulthood, the community began to grapple with its place in the order of things. It was a period of ecstatic indulgence and agonizing misery. Old bars and old problems faded away to make room for new bars and new problems. In the midst of these rapid changes, Café Lafitte in Exile remained constant, offering perspective and stability to the community. In this section we identify the influences that began to shape the gay community we see today in New Orleans.

Part Four - The 1980s: The Closet Door Falls Off Its Hinges

A Little Decadence Goes a Long Way

AS THE GLORY DAYS OF THE GAY CARNIVAL KREWES were reaching their peak in the early 1980s, another annual gay event was on the rise. Virtually all will agree the premiere gay event in the city now is Southern Decadence. Each Labor Day weekend, Decadence brings over 100,000 gays and lesbians to New Orleans and generates over $50 million in tourist revenue for the city. But in 1972, Southern Decadence was merely a way for a handful of bored college students to pass an uneventful weekend. They were several roommates sharing a slave quarters apartment behind a dilapidated house at 2110 Barracks Street in Tremé. Near the front door was a sign that read "Belle Reve," the name of Blanche DuBois' plantation in Tennessee Williams' *A Streetcar Named Desire*.

As Labor Day weekend 1972 approached, the residents of Belle Reve decided to have a farewell party for one of their own who was moving away. The party also served as a way "to shut up" a new arrival at the house, Maureen from Manhattan who constantly complained of the humidity and "having nothing to do." The theme of the party was "Southern Decadence." Guests were instructed to arrive dressed up as their favorite Southern decadent. About fifty people attended the party and a good time was had by all. According to Belle Reve resident Frederick Wright, it was "a good party, better than most, but nothing out of the ordinary" (Sears 97).

It was good enough for a repeat the following year. This time the Belle Reve revelers decided to inaugurate a parade. They began at Johnny Matassa's Grocery and marched back to Belle Reve, all the while dressed up as famous Southern decadents including, according to James Sears, Tallulah Bankhead, Belle Watling, and Mary Ann Mobley. For the third party, Wright was named Grand Marshall and the parade route was expanded to include The Golden Lantern, which remains the official headquarters of Southern Decadence. As the parade meandered around the lower Quarter, many people spontaneously joined the procession, including the late great

Ruthie the Duck Lady. The parade never has an official route; rather, it meanders around the Quarter at the whim of the Grand Marshall. This spontaneity is a source of much of the parade's energy and has created some unforgettable moments over the years. In 1986, Grand Marshall Kathleen Conlon led the parade to the Riverwalk where several drunken revelers jumped in the park fountains, much to the amusement and astonishment of throngs of tourists.[67]

The annual celebration grew slowly each year and by 1997, 50,000 gay people were coming to New Orleans each Labor Day weekend. The New Orleans Metropolitan Convention and Visitors Bureau began tracking Southern Decadence in that year and estimated the economic impact of the event in 1997 at $25 million. In 2003, Decadence drew over 120,000 visitors and $95 million to the city. By 2010, the number of revelers topped 130,000 with an economic impact of over $160 million. In recent years, Southern Decadence has replaced Mardi Gras as the biggest draw in the city for gay tourists. All the bars are constantly packed and many have cover charges. Lafitte's, proudly, does not.

The phenomenal growth of Southern Decadence has had a profound impact on the gay community in New Orleans in ways many people do not realize. More specifically, the success of Southern Decadence revealed to the straight community in New Orleans the spending power of the gay community long before the rest of the country realized that gay people were a powerful economic market with loads of expendable income.[68]

[67] Parts of this historical sketch of the origins of Southern Decadence have been adapted from James T. Sears landmark book, *Rebels, Rubyfruit, and Rhinestones.*

[68] For more information on the economic impact of the gay community we recommend Gluckman and Reed's *Homo Economics: Capitalism, Community, and Lesbian and Gay Life;* Badgett's *Money, Myth, and Change The Economic Lives of Lesbians and Gay Men;* Witeck and Combs' *Business Inside Out Capturing Millions of Brand Loyal Gay Consumers,* and Chasin's *Selling Out: The Gay and Lesbian Movement Goes to Market.* www.commercialcloset.org is an excellent online source of information as well.

Part Four - The 1980s: The Closet Door Falls Off Its Hinges

To be named a Southern Decadence Grand Marshall is one of the highest honors the gay community in New Orleans can bestow upon an individual.

Midgets, Poppers, and Whole Lot of DNA

AT THE DAWN OF THE 1980S, Café Lafitte was the place to go to get laid. The bar was consistently packed and many men report losing their gay virginity in the bar. The crowd was primarily, but not exclusively, middle-aged to older men and a bit more leathery than it is now. It was one of the few bars, gay or straight, that welcomed African-Americans. Women and drag queens, however, were not allowed. When the men we interviewed were asked to describe Café Lafitte in the early 1980s, typical responses included "skuzzy," "hard-core," "edgy," "lots of action," and "scary" for the uninitiated. Everyone was having sex everywhere: on the pool table, in the bathrooms, in the "blow job corner," and even while sitting at the bar. At the time, the bar was covered in burlap riddled with strategically and conveniently cut holes for easy fellatio access. Wallace Sherwood, affectionately known as "Wally the Midget," always dressed as a rabbit for the Gay Easter Parade and was a regular fixture "behind the burlap." Eventually the burlap had to go because so many guys were catching crabs from it.

Lloyd Sensat, who was a local artist, historian, and tour guide, remembered Café Lafitte in the 1970s as "always packed" and "full of action." Like so many people in New Orleans, and especially like so many GLBT folk, Lloyd was not from New Orleans. He grew up in Crowley, a small town in the southwestern part of the state. He echoed the sentiments of many when he said that even as a small boy, he wanted to live in New Orleans—that he someday knew he would move to the city. After a stint as a teacher in Acadia Parish, he did move to New Orleans in 1976. The pull of the city was strong and he was encouraged by a friend in Crowley who told him, "If you want to be happy, you have to leave this small town." That was sage advice but the sage didn't have the courage to heed his own advice and confessed to Lloyd he planned to marry a girl because, "I don't have the strength."

As a teacher in Crowley, Lloyd would come to New Orleans on the weekends and hang out at Café Lafitte. After moving to the city, his sexuality and creativity flourished. He observes, "What really attracted me to the city was the architecture and history. Being gay was just a plus." A plus indeed; especially after serving in the military closet in Korea. With only two months left to serve, Lloyd was caught "in the act" with another man. Perhaps because of his sterling record of service or perhaps because his superior officer was also in the closet, he was admonished to "be more discreet." Lloyd and his partner, Gene Cizek, had been together for thirty-four years and was a fixture in the Marigny until Lloyd's death in 2011.

Lloyd recounted a memorable incident from Lafitte's:

> Gene and I were at one of our local watering holes during Carnival. A new bartender had been brought in for Carnival. We learned that he was a porn star! Last week, he was still in town and working at the bar. He was very friendly and we were talking. He asked, "Are you from here?" I gave him one of my business cards. He screamed, "Mr. Sensat! You taught me in the sixth grade!" Of course, we discussed everyone that we knew in Luling. They must be something in the water in St. Charles Parish! Isn't it a small world!

Lloyd passed away not long after we interviewed him. His life is a good example of the countless gay men who made and are making contributions to New Orleans. Unlike so many who had gone before, Lloyd's contributions to the city were recorded in an obituary article in *The Times-Picayune*:

> During his teaching career in Acadia and St. Charles parishes, he was named U.S. Art Educator of the year in 1988 by the National Art Education Association. In 1991, the Disney Channel dubbed him its Visual Arts Teacher of

the Year.

Mr. Sensat and Cizek established the Education Through Historic Preservation Program, in which students were assigned to historical sites to understand their art and architecture. For that project, the pair received the Honor Award in 1981 from the National Trust for Historic Preservation.[69]

Another patron, Chris, remembers his first visit to Café Lafitte on Halloween night, 1979. He and a friend were walking down Bourbon Street when the friend suggested they duck into Lafitte's to get some poppers. The bar was extremely packed and the two snaked their way to a back wall near the bathroom. There Chris beheld a man wearing nothing but spiked heels, a jock-strap, and a leather harness standing on a barstool swinging a ball and chain. Chris ran out the bar "scared as shit," but very intrigued. He returned shortly thereafter and has been a regular since.

Jeffrey Palmquist remembers his first Southern Decadence as a bartender:

> I was new so I got a shit assignment—the balcony bar. But it was okay for Decadence because it was packed. This guy standing at the bar was drinking a Bud Light and talking to his friends. When he ordered another beer, I asked him if he needed anything else. The guy reaches down and grabs another by the hair and pulls him to eye level with the bar and says, "Want anything?" The guy on his knees nods no and his head disappeared. Until then it had never occurred to me the man standing had been getting a blow job the whole time. I soon learned that was very common.

---

[69] Pope, John. "Lloyd Sensat, 66, Tour Guide." *Times-Picayune* 23 Feb. 2011

Sex in the bar is not as common as it used to be but it does occasionally still occur, primarily during Mardi Gras and Southern Decadence weekends. These trysts almost always occur upstairs, but every now and then, raw lust manifests itself downstairs as well. David, a bartender, recalls recently showing up for his shift to see the entire bar fixated by a drunken drag queen "taking it up the ass by a big trucker dude" near the DJ booth. Likewise, Jeffrey remembers a similar incident from a few years ago. "The bar was fairly busy and kind of noisy. Then as I was mixing drinks, I heard what sounded like applause, only it wasn't. By the fireplace, somebody was getting fucked so hard that the thrusts against his ass sounded like hands clapping."

All this gay sex was just too much for some Christians to take. In the mid 1990s, a local pastor, the Reverend Grant Storms, began protesting Southern Decadence and Mardi Gras. But more than simply protesting, Storms went into the gay bars and surreptitiously filmed random sex acts being performed and went to the local media with the tape. The local news stations ran stories on the issue but the city, for the most part, shrugged its shoulders and forgot about it. Then the national media got wind of the story, and the city and the bars were compelled to respond, at least perfunctorily.[70] This is why most gay bars in New Orleans now have a no cameras/no photography policy. Reverend Storms eventually faded away into obscurity until he resurfaced rather dramatically in 2011 when he was arrested for masturbating at a children's park in Metairie.[71]

Lafitte's has a long history as a cruise bar. Longtime regular Louis wryly observes: "Before The Phoenix, before Jewel's, there was Lafitte's." In the late 1960s and early 1970s, Lafitte's

---

[70] "'Christian Patriot' Targets Gay Mardi Gras." *ABCNEWS.go.com*. n.p. Web.
http://abcnews.go.com/Primetime/story?id=131924&page=1#.TtpS_2PNltM

[71] Purpura, Paul. "Jefferson Parrish Prosecutors File Obscenity Charges Against the Rev. Grant Storms." *Times-Picayune*. 28 March 2011.

was "the only leather/Levi's bar in town . . . and they didn't have any twink bartenders back then. They came later." Louis, sixty-four, in his own words:

> Back then, business pretty much dictated your private life. You'd see men at Lafitte's at night wearing denim and Ts or leather or sometimes nothing at all, but during the day, these same guys wore conservative suits and played it straight. One guy I used to hang out with is still a member of Rex. The place was always packed. How the Fire Department never shut the place down is beyond me. There was always a lot of feeling and groping. Clusters of naked men would gather in corners or in the bathroom. They would be piles of clothes along the wall or near barstools but no one worried about them being stolen because we all knew each other and we looked out for each other.
>
> Hustlers didn't come to Lafitte's because so much ass was being given away for free. It wasn't worth their time. There was this one kid, though, I do remember. He must have been in junior high and he'd hustle on the corner right outside The Clover Grill. The bouncers wouldn't let him in because he was too young. Nobody really paid much attention to IDs then, but I guess they had to draw the line somewhere. Anyway, the regulars at Lafitte's used to watch out for him and bring him Cokes. He may have gotten some business from the bar but I think it was mostly closeted men who would drive by and pick him up.
>
> I had grown up on the West Bank and in Mid-City near City Park. I knew I was gay when I was around eleven or twelve years old, but I acted straight. Everyone did back then. We were all so scared. I was even engaged for a while. When we went out, I couldn't wait to drop her off at her

house after the date and go to Lafitte's. I must have been twenty-one the first time I went. One time I was with a group of friends in the Quarter and we ended up Lafitte's and we all acted like we didn't know it was a gay bar, which seems kind of silly now. When we left, one them said loudly acting surprised, "Man, that was a gay bar!" Oh, and I once ran into my cousin at Lafitte's. When he asked me what I was doing there I said, "The same thing you are."

I never did get married; I liked to play around too much. I still love chicken.

Sometimes, random hookups lead to meaningful relationships. Bill, a twenty-five-year regular at Lafitte's, grew up in a small town on Bayou Lafourche about an hour outside of New Orleans. When he was a senior in high school, Bill went to Lafitte's and fell in love with the place; it was his first gay bar. As a veteran of the gay scene in New Orleans, Bill has been to many gay bars but he always stays loyal to Lafitte's: "When I first started coming to New Orleans on the weekends I checked a lot of bars and clubs. I liked Lafitte's because it wasn't pretentious. It wasn't trendy and it wasn't spur-of-the-moment. It just was. And it still is."

During Mardi Gras 2008, Bill met David. David, a local who had grown up in Metairie, saw Bill across the bar and sent him a drink. Then he went over and introduced himself. In a matter of moments, the two were upstairs on "the meat rack."[72] After an especially memorable blowjob, they decided to see each other again and have been together ever since.

The Plague

AS IN OTHER BARS ACROSS THE COUNTRY, widespread promiscuity

---

[72] A "meat rack" is a ledge/counter along the wall of a gay bar where men sit as they wait to be cruised.

came to a screeching halt with arrival of The Plague in the early 1980s.[73] AIDS decimated the gay population in New Orleans, especially the Quarter which has always hosted thousands of tourists on a daily basis. Chris reported his worst memory of that time was "going to too many funerals."

Because of its popularity as a tourist destination, HIV probably arrived in New Orleans in the mid to late 1970s, but the full scope of the AIDS crisis did not grip the gay community in the city until the mid 1980s. As in other urban areas, the disease decimated the gay community, especially the gay carnival krewes. The men we spoke with who were around then found this issue the most difficult to talk about. Some refused to discuss it at all. Just as many broke down in tears as they remembered those they lost. All conveyed the same sense of sadness and horror. Longtime Lafitte's bartender Willamena summed up everyone's feelings by simply stating, "It was a very, very difficult time."

Willamena estimates he lost "at least" 100 friends and acquaintances to AIDS:

> It was so bad you were afraid to answer your phone. I remember throwing away my address book because most everyone in it had died. It was horrible. No one knew what was going on and everyone was fearful. Charity Hospital had a separate floor for AIDS patients. Orderlies would set patient's meals outside the doors in the hall for fear of being in the same room with someone

[73] Since the outbreak of the epidemic through 2008 (the latest figures available from the Center for Disease Control), the state of Louisiana has reported 20,319 AIDS cases to the CDC, earning a ranking of 11th highest among all 50 states. Of those, 46.5% were among men who have sex with men, 20.9% consisted of heterosexuals, 20.5% were intravenous drug users, and 9.6% were intravenous drug-using men who also had sex with other men. According to www.statehealthfacts.org, in 2009, 1,295 people in Louisiana were living with a diagnosis of HIV. Federal funding for HIV/AIDS in Louisiana totaled $65,563,295, a mere 2.1% of the national disbursement.

infected. And visitors were forced to wear masks and gowns. You'd go to the hospital to visit a friend and be shocked at how sickly they looked but also at how many other people you knew were also patients. After a while it took a heavy toll on me. I became cold.

As he rattled off name after name of those who had passed he paused at the mention of his friend Roger Garber. His voice cracked, tears began to form in his eyes. "I'm sorry. I need a moment." Roger had been a childhood friend in Ohio who eventually followed Willamena to New Orleans. In 1988, Roger seemed to suddenly disappear. He had moved home to die within days of testing positive. As the disease progressed and his health declined, he called Willamena and asked him to come visit him in Ohio. Upon arriving, Roger's mother warned Willamena of Rodger's ghastly appearance so he wouldn't freak out when he saw him. The warning was futile. Roger was pale and gaunt and thin, his face sunken into his skull, much of its skin eaten away by the meds (AZT). Willamena lost it. After regaining his composure, they visited and reminisced and laughed and cried. Roger was a huge Bette Midler fan and told Willamena, "You'll always be the wind beneath my wings." He died a few days later.

Jerry Hocke, Albert Carey's partner of seventeen years, succumbed to the disease in 1989, three years after being diagnosed. Reflecting on that dark time, Albert reminisced:

> Jerry was a veteran (he had a bum leg due to a mortar attack in Vietnam) so he died at the VA hospital. The staff wouldn't even go in the room. They would set his tray of food on the floor in the hall right by the door. I'd bring it in and feed him. There really weren't any treatment options then. The only drug that seemed promising was AZT and that was $900.00 for a month's supply. We heard of some drug the FDA had not yet approved but it was available in Mexico. I even went down

there to get some but it didn't work. Of course, in
that predicament, you try anything.

The ramifications of the AIDS outbreak were utterly
devastating to the gay community in New Orleans, especially
since it was such an intimate community. New Orleans has
always been a big small town with the French Quarter a village
unto itself. In years past, before its uber-touristification, the
Quarter had a close-knit neighborhood feel: everyone—
neighbors and bartenders and shopkeepers—knew each other.
This camaraderie was even more tightly woven among the gay
community. This parochial bond made the AIDS outbreak in
the mid-1980s seem much more intense and acute than it did
in larger cities. Everyone knew people who had died or were
dying and no one knew exactly why. Nor did anyone know how
to handle the crisis. Widespread public ignorance of the nature
of the disease, particularly how it spread, caused a lot of fear.
Paranoia and sadness ruled the day. Dr. Jody Gates, a lesbian
and the administrator of a hospital at the time remembers the
struggle to keep up with the latest laws and treatment
recommendations. "The most important thing," she recalls,
"was to not let people panic."
The gay community's reaction to the crisis was as diverse as
the community itself. Some men went back into the closet
while others vowed to be celibate. Some questioned all the
strides made in the previous decade and some even bought into
the conservative right's rhetoric of Divine judgment. Shame
and fear was a common reaction. Just as common was a
renewed determination to fight on for equality and dignity.
Doctors refused to see patients they knew were gay until they
were tested. Police used masks and gloves when arresting
known gay persons. Accounts differ on the lesbian
community's reaction to the outbreak. Several men we
interviewed recalled that many lesbians reacted with
indifference thinking, "It's not our problem." Still others
remember the lesbian community really stepping up to the
plate. Marcy Marcell hosted the first AIDS fundraiser in New
Orleans in 1984, raising about $350.00. Marcy recalls, "I was

at an Uptown party when CNN broke the story of a gay disease. We had no idea it would be as bad as it was."

Those infected reacted in different ways also. Some who became infected turned their anger into vengeance and tried to infect as many others as possible. Many went home to die. Some, who had no home to go home to, moved in with friends for their final days. Others went to die at Lazarus House, the first AIDS hospice in New Orleans (founded in 1985) and the oldest facility offering assisted living to AIDS patients in the Gulf Region.[74] According to Willamena, one victim, Patrick Kelly, decided to make the most of his remaining time by maxing out his credit cards and traveling the world. Others became hysterically convinced the virus was created and spread by the government to rid society of homosexuality.

In addition to the Lazarus House, other non-profit organizations emerged after the onset of The Plague to help fight the disease, notably: the NO/AIDS Task Force Community Awareness Network, HIV411.org (an excellent source for information and resources), Belle Reve (another AIDS assisted living program), Southeastern Louisiana AIDS Awareness, and the Saints and Sinners Literary Festival—an annual conference of editors, publishers, writers, and readers of GLBT literature. Local physician Dr. Brobson Lutz, considered by many to be the "Surgeon General of New Orleans" led the early charge in the fight against HIV/AIDS. Specializing in internal medicine and infectious diseases, Dr. Lutz has been at the forefront in vaccine research.

Willamena was (many would say miraculously) spared the virus, but as he notes, it took its toll on him in the horrifying deaths of so many of his friends. For his part, Willamena transformed his grief into the strength required to reconcile with his father. One day in 1986 he showed up unexpectedly on his parents doorstep and told his father firmly, "This ends now because it's only hurting Mom." Father and son embraced and began the process of restoring their relationship.

---

[74] For more information on Lazarus House, visit http://www.projectlazarus.net/

Part Four - The 1980s: The Closet Door Falls Off Its Hinges

Despite the devastation and heartache the AIDS crisis engendered, it did have one positive effect that is often overlooked: it humanized the gay community, which in turn affected many straight people's view on homosexuality. Looking back on those dark days, Jack Sullivan observes, "AIDS forced so many people out of the closet, the mainstream establishment realized, 'Oh, I didn't know you were gay.' AIDS created a forced visibility." Assessing the epidemic in hindsight, local businessman and former journalist Eric Hess simply, yet profoundly, observes, "AIDS changed everything."

Bartenders, Drug Addicts, and Other Characters

IF ANYTHING, NEW ORLEANS IS A TOWN OF CHARACTERS. Some eccentric, some criminal, some crazy, many all three or some combination thereof. All colorful. All revered. New Orleans has always embraced those of whom other cities demand bland conformity; the odder, the more eccentric you are in New Orleans, the more you fit in. And if you are an old soul, or even a young soul that can be described as "a character," you're not only accepted, but also appreciated. Uniqueness (especially of dress and speech) is celebrated; individuality worshipped, if you will. Throughout its storied past, Café Lafitte has played host to denizens of unconventional personalities, not the least of which include the bar's own employees.

Ken GrandPré, current manager of Wood Enterprises, estimates Lafitte's has gone through at least twenty managers in the last eighteen years. The number of recycled bartenders is much, much higher, easily in triple digits by all accounts. Several managers were petty larcenists, one even leaving a note in the safe on his last night that read, "I stole $400.00. Bye." Jerry Menefee opened The Caverns with liquor he allegedly stole from Lafitte's. And one manager in the early 1990s routinely raided the bartender's cash drawers in order to supply his coke habit. Several men told us of a bartender who stole "a lot of money" and allegedly fled to Brazil.

Hundreds of bartenders came and went at Lafitte's over the years but a few names came up repeatedly in our interviews, notably Alabama Jim, Billy Bayou, and Floyd. In addition to serving drinks, Floyd also orally serviced patrons—and he wasn't the only one. For a while, bartenders upstairs worked in the nude.

Lafitte's was not immune to the cocaine rage that swept the nation's nightclubs in the 1980s and 1990s. Joel Hoffman used to hide coke under his wig while he tended the bar in the mid-1990s. Hoffman went on to meet a tragic end, eventually overdosing from shooting up. Sadly, his body was found lying on the floor of an adult bookstore. One DJ in the 1990s sold coke out of the DJ booth but that little enterprise ended when the police came looking for him. They arrived at shift change and he was in the back of the house. Upon being alerted of their arrival, he hid in the walk-in cooler. The police, not realizing it was shift change, interrogated the DJ who had just come on duty. This DJ, not having anything to fear, answered all their questions and readily allowed them to search his bag. The police didn't find any coke but they did find a bundle of joints, which the poor DJ had completely forgotten about. Both DJs were arrested.

Robbie and Herbie, a couple that frequented the bar in the early 1980s, remember doing poppers at the bar one night when one of them dropped the bottle on the floor. As they crouched down, Robbie lit a cigarette lighter to look for the wayward bottle. In the process, the burlap caught fire. Regulars who were around then universally agree drugs were available everywhere.

Several bartenders used to openly snort rails of coke on the bar, as did some patrons, but for the most part, drug use at Lafitte's was invisible. The exceptions to this invisibility were two regulars Big Rick and his lover James who frequented the bar in the mid-1990s. The two were notorious drug users who, in 1998, bought Voodoo on Rampart Street one block from The Ninth Circle.

Perhaps because Lafitte's has no dance floor, and perhaps because the popular twink bar Oz is only a block away, Lafitte's managed to escape the meth craze that became popular at the turn of the millennium. This is not to say, of course, that

Part Four - The 1980s: The Closet Door Falls Off Its Hinges

Crystalina never visits Lafitte's; surely she does, along with the white bitch, Graham Greene, Mr. X, and their various associates. But for the most part, drug dealing and consumption is frowned upon in the bar these days.

Some people don't need to do drugs to be characters. Take for instance Cary, whose prosthetic leg had a propensity to fall off when he got drunk. Whenever the leg went AWOL, long-time bartender Aletha would scream at him as he stumble-hopped around the bar because other drunken patrons tended to trip over the wayward leg as it rolled around the floor. And then there was the house-painting drag queen who, in a drunken stupor, passed out and broke a bottle of Hot Damn in the process, which caused everyone to think (s)he was bleeding to death.

Ambush

ONE OF THE MORE SUCCESSFUL YELLOW BRICK ROADS in recent Quarter history is the path carved by Rip and Marsha Naquin-Delain, owners and publishers of *Ambush* magazine. Rip grew up in rural South Louisiana and attended college at Nicholls University in Thibodeaux. There he joined a fraternity but would occasionally sneak off to New Orleans with some gay friends on the weekend. The first time he set foot in a New Orleans gay bar he was a bit overwhelmed and became so scared his fraternity brothers, many of whom were from New Orleans, would find out he ran out the bar and took a bus home. He finally came out when he was twenty-one and when he did, his father told him, "You're gonna end up like those queers in New Orleans who burned,"—a not so subtle reference to The Upstairs Lounge fire. The first time Rip brought Marsha (Marty) home, his dad told him, "Don't you ever bring him home again!" Rip's reaction? "I didn't speak to my family for ten years." Marsha's coming out was less painful. Marsha grew up in Baton Rouge and came out to her mom when she was fifteen. Mom, a police officer, was incredibly supportive but they agreed it best not to tell dad, a local high school football coach. Marsha's mother used to drop him off at the gay bars so he could explore "the lifestyle" and even introduced him to her hairstylist, who became Marsha's first boyfriend.

Rip and Marsha met in 1974. They met one weekend in New Orleans and shortly thereafter moved in with each other. They were living in Baton Rouge when they started two gay publications that ultimately failed. The third time, as they say, was a charm. In 1982, they started their third magazine and called it *Ambush*. Originally, the magazine covered Baton Rouge and North Louisiana but was expanded to include New Orleans when they moved to the city in 1985. *Ambush* now serves the entire Gulf Coast gay community from Lafayette to Pensacola. Today the weekly magazine prints 10,000 copies of each edition and boasts a readership of 25,000, with several thousand more online readers.

Part Five
The 1990s and 2000s: Yellow Brick Roads Emerge from the Closet

THE LAST TWENTY YEARS in the New Orleans gay community have been a time of ripening and harvesting. The toil and labor of earlier activists began to bear fruit during this era and in the process began to gradually change the role and nature of gay bars. With homosexuality enjoying more cultural acceptance than it ever had before and with the ascendancy of the Internet, gay bars became de-centered as the focal point of gay life. Café Lafitte was emblematic of this trend, evolving from mysterious cruise bar to welcoming neighborhood bar. In this section we investigate early victories in the struggle for civil rights as well as various segments of the community outside the bar circuit.

On Balconies

IN 1995, LAFITTE'S STIRRED UP A BIT OF CONTROVERSY when bar owner Tom Wood proposed adding a metal roof to the balcony. When the Vieux Carré Commission met to consider the proposed changes, several neighborhood residents spoke out in opposition. In an effort to foster an honest dialogue, Wood wrote a letter to the roof's opponents urging them to speak with him directly about their concerns. The letter also stated, "We are glad for your participation in the community . . . and are glad to know who you (are) and where you live."[75] The quote was interpreted by some as a threat, a charge Wood denied. Opponents said they were worried the roof would amplify the noise coming from the bar. Wood claimed it wouldn't and might actually help muffle the noise. He then went on to claim their opposition really stemmed from homophobia. In a letter to the Commission, he wrote, "As for those who long for the days when our community was closeted behind closed doors and shutters, I have only pity. Is this issue really about noise and architecture, or our increasing visibility?"[76] Whatever it was about, the Commission voted five to one against the roof. The episode is emblematic of where the gay community was in its growth at the time: confident and mature enough to assert itself, yet still facing obstacles and opposition.

In the early years of Wood's tenure as owner, many regulars preferred the balcony bar to down stairs because it tended to be quieter and less crowded. Louis recalls the music being not as loud as it was downstairs, "You could actually talk to people upstairs. It was a great spot for conversation. And sex. We used to have a lot of sex upstairs, but that was usually on the weekend or for Mardi Gras."

---

[75] Warner, Coleman. "Proposed Roof on Bar Balcony Stirs Up Trouble." *Times-Picayune*. 14 Sept. 1995.

[76] Warner, Coleman. "Roof on Bar's Balcony Rejected." *Times-Picayune*. 20 Sept. 1995.

There is something special about French Quarter balconies and the balcony at Lafitte's is no exception. Multitudes of men have recounted for us memorable escapades on the balcony, especially during Mardi Gras and Decadence weekends. Typically on those weekends, sheets are draped over the iron work in order to somewhat conceal what can justifiably be described as an orgy of fellatio. Before Katrina, the balcony bar was open all week long, now it is only open on the weekends. Often, the balcony serves as a tranquil respite from the hustle and bustle of the main bar. Scotty, a longtime regular, says the balcony is his favorite spot in the city when it's not crowded:

> More than anything, I feel peace when I'm there. Sometimes Michael and I go there to sit and talk and relax and people-watch. I remember once I had a very stressful day at work and Michael said to me, "You need the balcony. Let's go to Lafitte's." So we went to unwind. It's so beautiful when the sun is setting. The taller, more modern buildings of the Central Business District silhouette the Spanish architecture of the buildings immediately before you. On that night, above the skyscrapers, the stars seemed to dance around a not-quite crescent moon and I totally zoned out. Michael waved his hand in front of my face to bring me back to earth and then asked me where I was. Then I was reminded why they call New Orleans "The City that Care Forgot."

Legal Strides in the 1990s

WHILE THE EARLY 1980S witnessed a flurry of gay organizing, anti-discrimination laws would take another decade to materialize. In 1991 the City Council finally passed a proposal to include "sexual orientation" as a protected category in an anti-discrimination ordinance.[77] Also in 1991, the city of New Orleans Mayor's Advisory Committee on Lesbian and Gay Issues published a report entitled *Exposing Hatred*. Based on a 1989 survey of 400 members of the GLBT community, the report is a fascinating survey of the officially sanctioned and freelance homophobia gays and lesbians faced at the time.[78]

In 1993 the city enacted a domestic partnership ordinance.[79] Five years later, the city council amended the 1991 statute to add "gender identity" as a recognized, protected class. New Orleans was one of the first American cities to do so. In 1997, Mayor Marc H. Morial extended domestic partner benefits to city employees.[80] In recognition of the longstanding contributions gays and lesbians have made to New Orleans, the city announced an outreach program designed to entice gays to move to New Orleans (Batson). Also in 1999, a state appeals court struck down Louisiana's long standing sodomy law[81] (enacted in 1805), which criminalized oral and anal sex.[82]

---

[77] Ordinance #19278, Sec. 54-379, New Orleans Code of Ordinances, Part II, Chapter 86, Article IV.

[78] See Magill, Rich. In addition to statistics on hate crimes, discrimination, and gay demographics, the report also includes personal testimonies of many people who recount their own struggles with indifferent or hostile police.

[79] Ordinance #19278, Sec. 87-5, New Orleans Code of Ordinances, Part II, Chapter 87, Article IV.

[80] Ordinance #19278, Sec. 87-9, New Orleans Code of Ordinances, Part II, Chapter 87, Article IV.

[81] *Digest of the Penal Law of the State of Louisiana Analytically Arranged,* (New Orleans: M.M. Robinson, 1841), page 142, Art. CCXXXVII, enacted May 4, 1805 as referenced by George Painter in *The Sensibilities of our Forefathers The History of Sodomy Laws in the United States.* http://www.glapn.org/sodomylaws/sensibilities/louisiana.htm

[82] New Orleans has traditionally been more progressive than the rest of Louisiana with regard to civil liberties but it bears noting that in 1997, Louisiana became the first state in the Deep South to pass a hate crimes law (RS 14:107.2) that included sexual orientation. Also, in 1992, Governor Edwin Edwards issued an executive order prohibiting discrimination in

In spite of the legal strides made by the gay community in the 1990s, a homophobic relic from previous decades reared its ugly head in 1998—the good old-fashioned police raid of a gay bar. Two days before Southern Decadence, police raided The Phoenix and arrested fourteen men, including the bar manager who was charged with permitting sexual acts to occur in a public facility that serves alcohol. It is believed to be the last raid of its kind.

By the dawn of the 1990s, public attitudes toward homosexuality had begun to change for the better. In 1990, Angela Hill of television station WWL hosted a week-long special series on the gay community in New Orleans. The five episodes each featured an aspect of GLBT life: What is homosexuality?, Do gay people in New Orleans face discrimination?, Should gay people be allowed to marry?, What are the common misconceptions of lesbianism?, and lastly, What problems do gay teens face? Each show featured three to five guests who answered questions from Hill and then the audience.[83]

An Afternoon at the Faerie Playhouse

AT 1308 ESPLANADE AVENUE stands a Creole cottage built in 1842. A rainbow gay pride flag graces the roof along with a sign that reads "Peace on Earth." On the outside wall is a plaque:

The Faerie Playhouse
1308 Esplanade Avenue

---

state employment and services. ("A Rich Gay Heritage" http://www.neworleansonline.com/neworleans/glbt/glbt-heritage.html)

[83] The twenty guests who appeared on the series were: Stewart Butler, Ruth Coker, Leif Eric, Susan Forester, Rev. Shelly Hamilton, Angela Hammond, Lynn Harper, David Indest, Joan Ladner, Dr. Lovelady, Marilyn McConnell, Loretta Mims, Jim Pepitone, Rich Sacher, Charlene Schneider, Mary Stewart, Dr. Douglas Webster, Judith Wenger, Curtis Yenigus, and an unidentified woman who wished to remain anonymous for fear of losing her job.

This Creole Cottage became the home of Stewart Butler and Alfred Doolittle in 1979 and was the site of many organizational meetings in the lesbian, gay, bisexual, and transsexual civil rights movement during the late 20th Century and early 21st Century. The garden behind this home contains the remains of many significant leaders in that struggle for equality, including Charlene Schneider, John Ognibene, and Cliff Howard, as well as artist J.B. Hartner.[84]

The Bienville Foundation
2007

I (Frank) am about to ring the bell when I notice the flag hanging from the eave which reads "End the War." Just then, the alley gate opens. There before me is Stewart Butler with his two dogs—Putz, an English Springer spaniel, and Holly, a mix. All three give me a warm greeting and Stewart ushers me inside for his interview. As Stewart gives me a brief tour of the house, I am struck by all the old photographs and original artwork, much of it by Stewart's partner of thirty-five years, Alfred Doolittle.

He points out photographs of Peter and Robbie, two teens he and Alfred took in as their own in 1988 and 1987 respectively. As he reminisces, I am struck by Stewart's appearance. He is not very tall but has a soothing, commanding presence. He is eighty years old but still very sharp. His shoulder length hair emanates from a velvet fishing hat of purple and gold. His eyes are gentle and blue and his facial features remind me of Benjamin Franklin. His red T-shirt bears the words: "Use me, Dump me, Crush me, Melt me, Use me again. Glass recycles." Around his neck are three

---

[84] Harter's name on the plaque is misspelled.

necklaces: one with a peace sign, one with a cross, and one with Reggae colors and a marijuana leaf. He strikes me as a gay wizard-guru-sage. As Stewart pours the coffee, he tells me, "There are many spirits in this house," and I believe him.

First we talk about Alfred, who recently passed away. "I met Alfred at Lafitte's in 1976. He looked just like Prince Valiant. As I was taking him home, he said to me, 'You'll probably throw me out tomorrow like the rest of them.' But I didn't." Alfred, whom Stewart describes as "a mental psychotic," was a writer as well as an artist who composed poetry and three plays, one of which, "Peter Puck," was performed one evening in the courtyard. "That's why it's called the Faerie Playhouse."

We sit at the dining room table and the memories begin to flow. He says:

> I went to LSU in 1947. I had a friend there who was gay and one day he told me that I was gay. I didn't come out for another thirteen years . . . I was born in Mobile and we moved to New Orleans when I was two. During the depression I had a 25¢ a week allowance . . . I lived in Carville a while and after school I joined the army. . . Spent about ten years in Alaska and returned to New Orleans in 1965 . . . We've had a lot of organizational meetings around this table.

He recalls one memorable LAGPAC Board meeting in the early 1970s at which Henry Schmidt, who was a member of DIGNITY (an unsanctioned Roman Catholic gay support group) lobbied for LAGPAC's endorsement of a boycott of Café Lafitte and other bars for discouraging women and African-Americans from entering their premises. The Board rejected their appeal by saying boycotts were not in their mission statement. But the real reason they rejected the boycott is because Tom Wood and Jerry Menefee were dues-paying members of LAGPAC and allowed the group to gather information for mailing lists in their establishments.

Years later, Stewart, ever the political activist, was fighting before the city council to have the transgendered community included in the sexual orientation protection ordinance the city had recently adopted. He enlisted the aid of the local Human Rights Campaign chapter, and when they rebuffed him, Stewart wrote to the national HRC office to ask why they were neglecting to defend the transgendered community. They wrote him back saying, "It's not in our mission statement."

"I suppose you really do reap what you sow," Stewart laughingly observes.

In addition to working with LAGPAC, Stewart has also been involved with Celebration, three national Marches on Washington, and continues to serve on the local PFLAG Board. Commenting on the current apathy with regard to gay political activism, he laments, "It's a bloody shame."

Concluding his interview, Stewart recounts his experience as a juror in criminal court in the 1990s. The trial involved two men who were charged with having public sex. "Everyone on the jury voted to convict, but not me. I hung it."

Gay Life Outside of the Bars

VIRTUALLY ALL OF THE MEN WE INTERVIEWED who were not natives of New Orleans but moved to the city as adults commented on the invisibility of the gay community outside the bars or Mardi Gras. Artist Skylar Fein, who grew up in Philadelphia and later lived in New York before moving to New Orleans, observes:

> In Philly the gay community is galvanized and well organized. There are gay sports leagues, gay meetings of all kinds, gay this and gay that, but not in New Orleans. There is a total absence of political activism but it's benign...Gay apathy is part of a larger culture. If we really wanted it, we would make it.

This observation is echoed by straight transplants as well. Bartley Mulligan, a local bartender who lived in New York for twenty years notes:

In Exile

I lived in the New York area from 1990 to
2010—the first four years of the '90s I was a
college student in New Brunswick, NJ. A few of
my best friends were in school in Manhattan so I
spent a good deal of time in NYC. Once I moved
to NYC I lived in Astoria for a few years, and then
moved into the Meat Packing District in
Manhattan, prior to its gentrification. I spent a
few years on the West Side, and then moved over
to the Lower East Side for a few more years. The
final ten or so years I lived in New York I was in
Brooklyn, first in Williamsburg, and finally
in Prospect Heights. It's kind of a New York thing
to identify the specific neighborhood you have
lived in, as if where you live says something
meaningful about who you are. When I lived in
the Meat Packing I worked in Soho so I walked
through the West Village to work every day. There
weren't many services in the Meat Packing (other
than tranny prostitutes who sometimes hung out
on my stoop) so most of my shopping was done in
Chelsea or the West Village.

Gay is everywhere in Manhattan, particularly
in the strongholds of Chelsea and the West
Village and north to Hell's Kitchen (Clinton as
real estate folk would have it) and south through
Soho. Rainbow flags are common as are
restaurants, bars, and businesses obviously
catering to GLBTT folk. Same-sex couples walk
the streets holding hands with little to fear in the
aforementioned neighborhoods. I'm not going to
claim that NYC is a gay paradise, but it's
definitely a good place to be openly gay. NYC has
an openly gay city council president, which is
progress from having an open secret closeted gay
mayor.

So, my experience in NYC was a gay

community that included an open, proud, sometimes in-your-face population, as well as an older, more sedate crowd, that, so far as I knew, did not advertise their sexual preferences, but felt no need to hide them.

As a new resident in New Orleans, I haven't seen the same sort of obvious gay community that was impossible to miss in NYC. I don't spend much time in the Quarter, which I understand is where the gay bars are, and perhaps if I lived down there, I would have a different perspective—but I live in MidCity where the flags are for Mardi Gras, LSU and Jazzfest. I know there's a Southern Decadence weekend, but I don't know if there's a gay advocacy group. Things are different here, to be sure, and I wonder how much of that has to do with continued traditions of open secrets and unspoken understanding.

Are these impressions accurate? Yes and no. Of course there are many gays who do not frequent the bars or are not involved in the gay Mardi Gras Krewes, but their visibility is limited to their own spheres of influence—neighbors, friends, and co-workers. Depictions of gay life in the straight media are typically confined to the economic impact of Southern Decadence, the gay Easter Parade, and, to a lesser extent, gay Mardi Gras. The only gay media to speak of is the *Ambush*, which focuses heavily, although not exclusively, on the bar scene. The Big Easy Metropolitan Community Church boasts a membership of eighty and hosts around fifty weekly worshipers. The GLBT Community Center sponsors a book club, a transgender support group, and a young men's social group that discusses AIDS prevention.

With such a large gay population, one would think New Orleans would host a vibrant Pride celebration each June but such is not the case. According to a former Pride Committee member:

Gay Pride never caught on due to Southern Decadence. Most tourists think that SD is our pride. Also they want pride in June which is usually too damn hot. By having Pride in June, it competes with the larger prides such as New York and Atlanta. We had a large parade and also live entertainment, various vendors, a drag stage, riverboat cruise, pride week, Dyke March and Dance tents. These happened while we were at Armstrong Park. The largest amount of attendance was about 3,000 people during the weekend. When we were at Washington Square Park attendance was about 1,500.

Radical Faeries

ONE OF THE MORE INTERESTING MANIFESTATIONS of the gay community in New Orleans is The Radical Faeries.[86] In 1979, Harry Hay, who had earlier founded the Mattachine Society, and his partner, John Burnside, founded the Radical Faeries with this call to "gay brothers everywhere:"

---

[86] "Radical Faeries (also Faeries and Faes) are a loosely affiliated worldwide network of people seeking to reject hetero-imitation and redefine queer identity through spirituality. The Radical Faerie movement started in the United States among gay men during the 1970s sexual and counterculture revolution. The movement has expanded in tandem with the larger gay rights movement, challenging commercialization and patriarchal aspects of modern LGBT life while celebrating pagan constructs and rituals. Faeries tend to be fiercely independent, anti-establishment, and community-focused. Faerie culture is undefinable [sic] as a group; however, it has similar characteristics as "Marxism, feminism, paganism, Native American and New Age spirituality, anarchism, the mythopoetic [sic] men's movement, radical individualism, the therapeutic culture of self-fulfillment and self-actualization, earth-based movements in support of sustainable communities, spiritual solemnity coupled with a camp sensibility, gay liberation and drag." (Source: Wikipedia.com)

To share new insights about ourselves,
To dance in the moonlight,
To renew oaths against patriarchy, corporations
and racism,
To hold, protect, nurture and caress one another,
To talk about the politics of gay enspiritment and
the enspiritment of gay politics,
To find healing space inside our hearts,
To become the inspirer and the listener as we
share new breakthroughs in how we perceive
gay consciousness,
To soar like an eagle,
To rediscover and reinvent our myths,
To talk about gay living and loving alternatives,
To experience the groundedness of the calamus
root,
To share our gay visions,
To sing, sing, sing,
To evoke a great fairy circle.[87]

Many responded to the call and before long the Radical Faeries were a loosely affiliated international organization, the New Orleans group being organized in 1990. Today the New Orleans Faeries sponsor a number of activities including annual Mardi Gras and Southern Decadence Balls and a potluck supper each Wednesday night.

Recently I attended a Faerie potluck dinner at the home of independent documentary film-maker Tim Wolff. Here is my (Frank) journal entry describing the event:

> Wednesday night, Feb. 9—very cold and rainy. Heading north on St. Claude for Faerie potluck on Marais near Poland Ave. The house is old but spacious and exudes that quality of decayed elegance for which New Orleans is known. About

---

[87] http://groups.yahoo.com/group/NOLAFaeries/

25 people are gathered—none of whom I have ever met—in the kitchen and various rooms drinking wine and beer and chatting. Tim shows a few of us a promo of *The Sons of Tennessee Williams*, a documentary he made of Gay Mardi Gras which is to air next week on WYES. Everyone is friendly and eager to speak with me when they learn I'm not an FBI agent gathering information but rather amassing research for a book.

First I speak with Clay, who has just come from a community meeting about crime in the St. Roch neighborhood. Last week he presided as the 22nd Empress at the group's Mardi Gras Ball. He laughingly declares, "That's how radical the radical faeries are; they made a straight man empress!" I then float around chatting with several faeries when I notice an altar. I am informed the altar is for Peter, a former faerie who passed away. Victory, a founding faerie, invites me to sit with him so he can tell me more about Peter.

Peter, I learn, worked for the enforcement arm of the Vieux Carré Commission. Victory describes him as "light . . . his charisma was larger than life . . . a peacemaker . . . made people feel up and alive and happy . . . he was a mover and shaker among faeries who loved to party." I also learn Peter was recently "elevated" to Faerie Sainthood. Victory references three miracles performed by Peter but does not elaborate on them. I ask about the faerie beatification process but no one seems to know the specifics.

Our conversation is interrupted by a "call to circle." All the faeries, and myself, form a circle and hold hands. Various faeries begin to make announcements. As this occurs several faeries begin to hiss faintly. Then we eat. After the meal,

Victory and I resume our conversation. Victory, who has the demeanor of a sage, offers to do a Tarot card reading for me. He does and begins to dispense life insights. The mind is the most abstract place in the cosmos . . .

King Cake Queens

ONE OF THE MORE POPULAR FEATURES of gay Mardi Gras is the annual bead toss sponsored by the Krewe of Queenateenas. During Mardi Gras, fifty men gather on the balcony of the *Ambush* magazine headquarters in the 800 block of Bourbon. The next year's Queen is determined by the Queenateena who successfully entices the most street revelers to show their dicks for beads. The winner is honored with a black-tie Coronation party. Throughout the year, the King Cake Queen participates in fundraising events for various charities throughout the gay community. After her year-long reign, the Queen is inducted into The King Cake Queen Royalty Club. According to Rip Naquin-Delain, the Krewe's co-founder, "The whole thing started as a joke."

If there is such a thing as the upper echelon of gay society in New Orleans, it can be found at the coronation party of the King Cake Queen, hosted annually at the "Ambush Mansion." In 2011, I (Frank) attended the event and recorded the following entry in my journal:

> The theme of the evening is "The Imperial House of Japan Boards the Orient Express." As I walk through the Quarter on my way to the soirée, the night is comfortable—not hot and not cold. The streets are bustling with revelers, more than usual no doubt because tonight Krewe du Vieux rolls. As I pass Good Friends, I notice a few tuxedo-clad elegants fortifying themselves at the bar in preparation for the social hour awaiting them around the corner.
>
> I approach the *Ambush* entrance and am

greeted by a police officer who kindly requests my invitation ticket. Entering the ancient alley, I am directed into the front room where I take my place in the receiving line. Across the room, King Cake Queen XVIII, Rona Conners (also known as "The Chrysanthemum Queen"), stands majestically in full Japanese royal drag regalia surveying and greeting her subjects. When my turn comes, I dutifully pose for a picture with her Royal Majesty, exchange pleasantries with the co-captains, and then proceed upstairs for the buffet.

At the top of the spiral staircase, which is lined with portraits of previous queens and various memorabilia from past Mardi Gras festivities, I find myself in another line, this one for the cocktail bar, which is being manned by a friendly face, longtime Quarter bartender, Ashley. Upstairs there are two rooms, a sitting parlor and a formal dining room which opens onto a balcony overlooking Bourbon Street. Many faces are familiar; many are not. There are the usual suspects from the bar scene and more than a few Uptown queens who would never be seen in the bars. I am first greeted by Paul, who serves as tonight's uniformed waiter. There is Toby, the reigning Grand Marshall of Southern Decadence. Other Grand Marshals are present too, some with glittering pins adorning their tuxedos signifying the year of their reign; ditto for the Queens of several gay carnival krewes. Rainbow-colored jewelry is in abundance, particularly fleur de lis'.

The buffet table is beautifully adorned in an Oriental motif, the grandeur of which is rivaled only by the food itself: Peking Duck & Gourmet Mini Sausage, Yamato Dynasty Sushi, Wild Boar Teriyaki, Imperial Oyster & Hog Pyramid, Pagoda Noodles with Rabbit, and Cream Cheese King Cake. The place fills up quickly and soon there is hardly room to move. Everyone is nibbling and chatting up close and personal. Wanting a brief respite from all the dazzling cuff links and overpowering colognes, I make a move for the balcony, but it too is jam-packed.

The story of the Krewe of Queenateenas and its resounding popularity is a prime example of how spontaneous events, especially something fun, in New Orleans have a tendency to take on lives of their own and become local institutions. French Quarter Fest, The Running of the Bulls, the Oak Street Po-Boy Festival, and Southern Decadence are other good examples.

One Does Want a Hint of Leather

SOUTHERN DECADENCE GRAND MARSHALL 2010, Toby Lefort grew up in the small town of Larose on the banks of sleepy Bayou Lafourche about an hour south of New Orleans. When he came out in high school, no one was really surprised and his family was very supportive. Eager to explore his sexuality, Toby went to his first gay bar (Kicks) in neighboring Houma and soon thereafter began frequenting The Full Moon in Destrehan. In 1992, he moved to New Orleans. As he witnessed his first Southern Decadence, he was struck with child-like wonder by the grandeur of the Grand Marshall and told his boyfriend at the time, "I wanna be that some day." It only took eighteen years. In the meantime, a friend, Travis, had succumbed to AIDS in 1997. Travis' struggle motivated Toby to get involved with the gay community, particularly AIDS fundraising. Before he died, Travis told Toby, "I want you to beat Rip and Marsha (in fundraising) in the NO/ AIDS Walk." Toby recalls, "That's how I became active in the community." In 2009, Toby began to explore the local leather community and in 2010 won the Mr. Louisiana Leather Contest. He went on to compete in the International Leather Contest and finished in the top twenty. Capping off a phenomenal year, Toby and a partner opened Club LAX in Metairie.

Toby and others in the leather community describe the

leather subculture as separate and distinct from mainstream gay culture. Toby explains joining the leather community a second coming out:

> I truly do feel that my interest in leather was a second coming out because it was a whole new ballgame. It's like people look at you like you are a freak but just because we like the leather culture we are the same person we were before.

The gay leather subculture that we know today originated in the California motorcycle culture that blossomed in the years just after World War II.[88] These early leather groups were not exclusively homosexual, and while rough sex play involving dominant and submissive roles was a factor, sadomasochism was not their defining characteristic. Partly influenced by the 1953 Marlon Brando film, *The Wild One*, California leather culture in the 1950s focused on codes of dress, hyper-masculinity, and a rejection of middle-class values. In the 1960s, a distinct gay leather culture emerged in New York and Chicago, manifesting itself primarily in leather bars and private clubs, and in the 1970s, bathhouses.[89]

The premiere leather organizations in New Orleans are The Lords of Leather and The Cavaliers, a gay motorcycle club. The Lords of Leather, founded in 1983, is the only gay leather carnival krewe in the world. There are two current leather bars in New Orleans, The Phoenix and Rawhide.

Santa Claus is Gay

---

[88] For those interested in the development of leather culture, we recommend Mark Thompson's book *Leatherfolk: Radical Sex, People, Politics, and Practice*, and Robert V. Bienvenue's article "The Development of Sadomasochism as a Cultural Style in the Twentieth Century United States."

[89] See Thompson. This historical survey of the development of the leather subculture is adapted from the introduction of Thompson's book.

Part Five - The 1900s & 2000s: Yellow Brick Roads Emerge From The Closet

ONE OF THE MORE INTERESTING CHARACTERS in the current gay landscape of New Orleans is Santa Claus. Seriously. The first man in the United States to have his name legally changed to Santa Claus lives in the French Quarter and he's a dead ringer for everyone's favorite end of the year sugar daddy. Of all the street performers who roam the Quarter on a daily basis, Santa is perhaps the most unique. Each day he walks the Quarter posing for pictures with locals and tourists alike, all the while collecting donations and spreading holiday cheer. In the summer, he dons red Bermuda shorts, red crocs, and a red Hawaiian shirt; on winter days he wears a full Santa suit— either the traditional red and white or a custom made black and gold Saints version. At the end of the year he makes multiple appearances at bars and restaurants around the Quarter raising money for Toys for Tots.

Now fifty-nine, Santa grew up in Kansas City, the ninth of thirteen children in a very Roman Catholic family. In junior high school, he and his playmates began experimenting with each other's bodies, thus satisfying a common curiosity among young teen boys. It wasn't until he went to college that he realized he was different:

> In high school, my friends moved on to girls but I never grew out of it. Before high school, I didn't realize that gay was different, that I should stay in the closet or even that there was a closet. I was just me. I was fairly athletic and was on the football and wrestling teams. I suppose you could say I was out at the time but that word didn't exist then. I never announced my sexuality but I didn't deny it either. For whatever reason, it just wasn't a big deal.

Santa, a member of MENSA, eventually earned an M.A. in psychology and went into sales. During his time as a realtor in Houston, Santa fell on hard times and eventually became homeless. Tired of living in his car and exhausting all opportunities in Houston, he drove to Atlanta, where he had enjoyed success in previous years. But the Peach City had gone sour and Santa remained homeless there for five years before deciding to return to Houston. Serendipitously, he ran out of gas in New Orleans. New Orleans received him with open arms and smiled broadly as it embraced him. Santa lived at the Salvation Army shelter for a year as he learned the city and perfected his craft as a street performer in the French Quarter, where he now lives in a very nice apartment.

So what's it like to be homeless and gay? In a word, difficult. Santa reports an anti-gay bias in many police officers, a bias which motivates these police officers to harass the gay homeless more than the straight homeless. As an example, he cites a friend who was arrested for violating an obscure law that prohibits a person from obscuring the flight path of a pigeon. The court system is not much kinder, often remanding the homeless person, whom they almost always assume to be an addict or alcoholic, to a mandatory rehabilitation program in a homeless shelter, often administered by a religious organization. Drawing from first-hand experience in the homeless shelters, Santa describes these programs as ineffectual and consisting exclusively of "God, shower, food."

Within the shelters there are cliques of young gays who are "obvious." These cliques are singled out and discriminated against in subtle and not so subtle ways. For example, they are the last to eat, have separate shower times and are generally shunned. "It's not the official policy, but it is the reality," Santa notes. Because of this shabby treatment, many gay youths who are homeless refuse to go to the shelters, preferring instead to live in packs on the streets. Santa concludes, "There is a tremendous need for a homeless shelter that caters to young gay people."

Katrina: The Gay Community Blows Back

JOHN GOTTHELF MOVED TO NEW ORLEANS on August 1, 2005 one month before Hurricane Katrina. Because his apartment in the French Quarter was on the fourth floor of an old warehouse that had been converted for residential use, he decided to stay and ride out the storm. Five days after the levees breached, he hitched a ride to Baton Rouge and eventually made his way to his sister's home in Alabama. What were those five days like?

> Fortunately I had lots of cigarettes, valium, and peanut butter. I was new in town and didn't really know what was going on. I had visited New Orleans before many times as a tourist but this was different. There was no running water and I stunk really bad. I was gone four weeks and came back as soon as I learned my block had power. Returning was surreal. It was mostly deserted and looked like a third world country. Trash was everywhere. Looking back, I probably returned too soon. But a few of the gay bars were open and that helped.

As the horrific consequences of the "Federal Flood"[90] unfolded over the next several weeks, many people questioned the wisdom of locating a city is such a low-lying, vulnerable area. What those people failed to realize is that the French Quarter, the original city, did not flood. They also fail to understand that in 1718, the year New Orleans was founded, locating a city here made perfect sense. Lake Pontchartrain and the Mississippi River are New Orleans' *raison d'être*. Early European settlers realized that controlling the mouth of the river meant controlling the interior of the continent. The mouth of the river's military and economically strategic location was obvious to the colonial powers of eighteenth century Europe. Historian Pierce Lewis writes the city was inevitable, even if the location was improbable.

Improbable indeed. Early colonial maps indicate *L'Île de*

---

[90] Many people in New Orleans refer to the flooding of New Orleans during Hurricane Katrina as the "Federal Flood" because if the levees, which were built and are maintained by the US Army Corps of Engineers—a Federal entity—had not failed, August 29, 2005 would have been just another rainy, windy day in New Orleans.

In Exile

Nouvelle Orleans, and, as John Maginnis notes, "an island it is" (115). New Orleans is surrounded by water—the Mississippi, Lakes Pontchartrain, Maurepas, and Borgne, the Barataria Bay, a labyrinth of bayous, thousands of acres of marshy swamp, and the Gulf of Mexico. All that water means flooding. From its inception, frequent flooding has always plagued New Orleans. The construction of levees and locks and spillways and pumps has helped a great deal but, as Katrina so dramatically demonstrated, all the civil engineering in the world is no match for Mother Nature when she's really determined to have her way. In addition to life-giver, water is also death-bringer, the enemy.

William Butler Yeats could have easily been writing about post-Katrina New Orleans when he penned the following lines in "The Second Coming":

> Turning and turning in the widening gyre
> The falcon cannot hear the falconer;
> Things fall apart; the centre cannot hold;
> Mere anarchy is loosed upon the world,
> The blood-dimmed tide is loosed, and everywhere
> The ceremony of innocence is drowned;
> The best lack all convictions, while the worst
> Are full of passionate intensity. (1-8)

As Katrina made landfall in the early morning hours of Monday, August 29, 2005. Javier, a fixture in the Quarter and the gay community since 1973, and about twenty others hunkered down at Starlight by the Park on North Rampart. None of them could have known the horrors about to befall New Orleans, but they started to get an idea when the wooden façade of the building was ripped away by the roaring winds. As the apocalypse unfolded over the next ten days, Javier, also known as Javi, emerged as an organizer and a leader:

> The day after Katrina was just beautiful, not a
> cloud in the sky. We met at Starlight and no one
> had a clue what was going on. Several queens

were planning to go to the Superdome but I talked them out of it. They would have never survived. The National Guard didn't arrive for four or five days, and when they did, they were outnumbered. It was all very Wild West, everyone fending for themselves. Some people were trying to steal money but that was pointless because money was worthless. Cigarettes were in high demand. I owned an apartment building on Dauphine at the time. Most of my tenants left. It became a sort of compound. We had gas so I opened a sort of soup kitchen. We also cooked and gave out water at Starlight, which was open during the day but closed up at night. Us and Johnny White's were the only bars to stay open through the whole thing.

One image I'll never forget is a man leading a group of people on the neutral ground walking from the 9th Ward to the Superdome. He had a baby in one arm and was holding another kid's hand and behind him was a group of people that looked like a bunch of zombies. We offered them bottled water and the look in his eyes was just so bleak. I'll never forget that.

On day six the flies became a real problem. There was obviously no garbage collection and the flies got really bad. We made homemade fly-swatters out of wire hangers, masking tape and window screen netting. We all had duties. Each person became responsible for something. We had to ration everything. We decided to wash our hair every four days with water from the hot water heater. Somehow, around day seven, someone produced two cups of ice we rationed out among us. That was a treat.

Two elderly ladies who lived across the street had stayed and I was concerned about them. A lot of older folks who stayed were running out of

In Exile

medication. Someone in the nursing home by the dog park must have money or pull or something because a bus came to get them with a state police escort. I stopped the driver to ask if he would take the two sisters but they didn't want to go. The trooper told me he would pretend his car had stalled and said I had twenty minutes to convince them to leave. They finally agreed and ended up leaving. That was on day five.

Some have said Southern Decadence was canceled but it wasn't. On Sunday, about thirty of us gathered at The Golden Lantern, not including the media. There was a lot of media. We marched to Johnny White's then we went to the compound to bar-b-que. Thank God for booze.

Javi is also thankful there was a lot of marijuana around:

A lot of people we knew who smoked left their weed behind. A dealer in particular. They weren't coming back any time soon and we needed it. So we helped ourselves to it. It was like a rebate for years of loyalty. I finally left on day ten. My mom called from Texas and told me I needed to come home. The city was on lock down and nobody could get in so I had to get to the Orleans/Jefferson line to be picked up. The whole experience was surreal. Everything you learn in the Boy Scouts about survival really came in handy. If I had to do it over again, I still would have stayed. I have no regrets. Life is too short for regrets.

The weeks and months after the storm were apocalyptic for those who stayed. Heath, a young hustler who was living in the Bywater at the time, remembers going out every few days in search of food and supplies. At the Robert's grocery store on Elysian Fields, he recalls police cracking open the ATM and stuffing the cash in their pockets, and then announcing to the crowd they should "take what you need. There will be no food in New Orleans for a while." About a month into the disaster, the National Guard knocked on Heath's door and asked him if he needed medical attention. Heath pointed out a cut in his leg he acquired while foraging for food in a destroyed store. Over his protests, the National Guard took him to the airport where, he was told, his injury would be treated. Instead, he waited in limbo for three days before he and about sixty others were put on a plane and sent to Tennessee. After three weeks there, Heath returned to New Orleans.

About a month after the storm, Lafitte's opened on a Wednesday and the number of people who came that night was truly amazing.[91] On that night, two drag queens, Tittie Toulouse and Lisa Beaumann, suggested the bar host a fundraiser for storm victims. The show was put together quickly and was scheduled for Friday. It was well attended at first but then the Bourbon Pub opened that night and nearly everyone left to go there. Wood and Gran Pre' countered by giving away free drinks, a move, which lured the crowd back. By the end the night, the bar raised $1,750 for Katrina relief.

After the storm, tourism fell off a great deal, which affected business at the bar, and many locals who had been regulars never returned. Some tried but said the memories of the flood were too fresh. Like New Orleans itself, Café Lafitte has slowly been building back up to its former glory. Old traditions such as Trash Disco on Sundays, Monday Movie Night, and Wednesday night karaoke have been restored and are going strong. When Trash Disco started in the 1980's, owner Tom Wood hated the napkin toss because napkins cost money. When he forbade their use, patrons made confetti by shredding old copies of *Ambush* and *Impact*. Karaoke night began in the 1990s after Tom and Ken met a Pro-Sing company representative during a trip to Las Vegas. Originally, karaoke

---

[91] Lafitte's, along with the French Quarter, remained undamaged. The Quarter did not flood although a few buildings sustained minor wind damage.

was held upstairs until it moved downstairs after Katrina.

Many in the GLBT community encountered homophobia while in exile after the storm. For example, Arpollo Vicks, a twenty-year-old transgendered woman also known as Sharli'e Dominique, was arrested by the Texas A&M University Police for using the women's shower facility at the evacuation shelter where she was deposited. She was charged with criminal trespassing and was held in the Brazos County jail for five days under a prohibitively high bail. After the incident received wide notice and she was released without charges, the Montrose Counseling Center in Houston arranged to house her and her family.[92]

Among the many Katrina casualties in the gay community was Rosemary "Mama" Pino, who owned and operated five bars during the 1970s and 1980s. The beloved community leader was eighty-three years old. She died of undetermined causes in a nursing home that was not evacuated in advance of the storm.

Community organizations were also damaged. Activists and other personnel were scattered across the country. Facilities and equipment were destroyed. With the city's economy shattered, the financial ability of supporters to rebuild the infrastructure of the GLBT community was also severely diminished. Many GLBT individuals and organizations around the country responded with aid to the beleaguered city, notably the National Youth Advocacy Coalition who provided grants for youths in need.

Perhaps the most significant untold story of Katrina and its aftermath is how the gay community essentially kick-started the French Quarter after the storm. All the gay bars and businesses were up and running within four weeks of the flood and many in the gay community stayed during the whole ordeal. A month after the storm, *The Advocate* ran a cover

---

[92] Hensley, Laura. "Transgendered Evacuee Released." *The Bryan-College Station Eagle*. 10 Sept. 2005

highlighting the effects of the flood on gay New Orleans.[93] The edition featured several short articles, including an optimistic piece by columnist Christopher Rice, and a cover story about two lesbians determined to return to the city and rebuild. Veteran Quarter bartender Will Antill says, "It's coming back."

Yellow Brick Roads

THE PATTERN IS FAMILIAR: gay youth comes out or is outed, gay youth leaves home (usually under duress), gay youth dives into bar culture, gay youth embarks on odyssey of self discovery. Every gay youth's yellow brick road takes different twists and turns but along the way there are universal commonalities—supportive friends, wicked witches, fantastical epiphanies, and ultimately, hopefully, contentment. Here are a few journeys.

Popular Lafitte's DJ Myke came out in 1979 at age nineteen. Upon discovering some poppers and a few gay magazines in his room, his mother, both sad and furious, called his father at work. Myke was asked to leave his house. Full reconciliation with his parents would take twenty years. A few years earlier, when he was seventeen, he had his first sexual experience with a man. He was working as a cashier at a store when an older man propositioned him. In 1980 he started making the rounds at the gay bars. He had been reluctant to go to the bars because of the movie *Cruising* staring Al Pacino. He found Café Lafitte's particularly "fearful" because it was "dark and mysterious."

Myke joined a rock band as lead singer and eventually married twice. Both women knew he was gay and he was with men while he was married. Both wives were sexually open-minded, the second in fact was a lesbian, and threesomes were a regular feature of both marriages. He had married in order to have children but that was not to be. Then Myke met Max, also a native New Orleanian. Max was married but not out. Not out, that is, until he was busted by his sister-in-law one day as she

---

[93] Hernandez, Greg. "Reviving New Orleans." The Advocate. 11 Oct. 2005: 49-52.

secretly followed him to Myke's. Myke and Max fell in love and have been together eleven years. They celebrated their life together in 2009 with a commitment ceremony.

Tim grew up in a small town in Ohio. Asked if he knew he was gay while growing up, he responded, "Everybody else probably knew but I didn't until I was in college." There he came out to a few friends and began finding his way. Then, one of his friends from college mailed him a few gay-themed magazines. His parents intercepted the mail and suddenly realized their suspicions were true—little Timmy was the boy they had hoped for. His father was surprisingly calm, asking him only if he was gay, to which Tim responded, "I don't know if I can say that yet." His mother was not so calm. In Tim's words, she "flipped out" and "didn't talk to me for a week." At the end of the week they had a heated discussion over the issue, his mother insisting that he seek psychiatric help. Tim held his ground and thus ensued ten years of stony silence between them:

> I pushed her away. I wanted to avoid the issue. After getting my degree I took a job in Mobile, Alabama. I was still not completely comfortable with myself and was not out at work. I did start dating a guy and we ended up moving to New Orleans together in 1992. We were together for three years but, I discovered, he had been cheating on me and taking advantage of me financially the whole time. He had re-opened credit card accounts I had previously closed and ruined my credit. He put me in a lot of debt. I confronted him and there was drama. I did kick him out but he continued to be an asshole to me. He moved in two doors down from me and one time he called me while I was at work and told me he was HIV positive. I later discovered he wasn't. I became really bitter and didn't trust gay men. If they approached me in the bars, I was a total bitch to them. I grew an attitude. I drank a lot and

started doing coke on the weekends.

I started going to Lafitte's because a bartender I liked got a job there. He didn't last long but I stuck around because I felt comfortable there. The crowd was a bit older, which was nice because at the pub, where I was hanging out before, I felt old. I preferred the upstairs bar at Lafitte's because it was easier to talk to people, the music wasn't as loud as it was downstairs and it was usually less crowded. Except on the weekends when people cruised the pool table area. I met my one and only one-night stand at the pool table. We called the guy Rodeo Bob because he said he was in town for a rodeo. We went to the ladies' rest room to fool around, and then we went to my place.

Tim went on to have one serious relationship that lasted seven years. They bought a place on the North Shore but eventually grew apart. Tim has sense moved back to the city and is an active volunteer with the NO/AIDS Task Force.

Heath arrived in New Orleans four months before Hurricane Katrina. Nineteen years old and directionless, he checked into the Covenant House, a homeless shelter for young adults aged sixteen to twenty-four. There Heath earned his GED and settled into life in New Orleans until he was expelled because of a conflict with another resident. On the streets he learned of the Ozanam Inn, another homeless shelter which afforded men nighttime lodging but required them to leave during the day. One day as he walking the Central Business District in search of a job, a man in a truck, a contractor, pulled over and asked him if he wanted to work. After the day's work, the man offered Heath a place to stay—and money for sex.

It was the first time Heath had ever had sex with a man. Having grown up in a deeply religious family, Heath had always thought of himself as straight. He had lost his virginity to an older female prostitute a few years earlier and had dated girls:

In Exile

Growing up, I knew gay existed but I didn't really know what it meant. When I was fuckin' around with Dave, it was all about the money and having a place to live. There was no emotion to it at all. The first time he fucked me in the ass I was scared shitless. But I liked it. I ended up staying with him for about a year.

They stayed during Katrina, and in the months afterward, they worked construction jobs constantly:

The work was steady and the money was awesome. I learned roofing and how to install electrical systems. That was cool 'cause it was a skill. Things were going great until Dave screwed me over by paying me with bad checks. After a lot of drama I ended up back on the streets. One afternoon I was walking down Rampart Street when a woman invited me into a bar called Starlight. After a while, I realized she was actually a he. That was the first time I ever saw a tranny. She paid me to suck my dick and we ended up becoming friends. I ended up moving in with her and got a job bar-backing at the Starlight.

The whole time I had a girlfriend. She had no clue I was with guys. She did find out later, and then we broke up. I like tits a lot which I guess is why it was easy to have sex with trannys—I could look at their tits while getting fucked. It was during that time that I got to know the gay bars. I had never been in a gay bar before. I liked it because I felt accepted more than I ever had. I mostly hustled out of The Doubleplay. It was an easy way to make quick money, which came in handy because I'm addicted to video poker. Most of the time tricking scared the shit of me because I did it without protection. I did get tested regularly though.

I ended up moving in with an ex-marine for a while but he treated me like shit. I also worked in a bunch of restaurants. In 2008 I went to Lake Charles with a guy I tricked with and ended up staying there five months. I got a job working at McDonalds, which was good, but I also started smoking crack. After a while of that I knew I had to get out of there. I spent my last paycheck on a bus ticket and came back to New Orleans.

Back in New Orleans, Heath went to rehab and kicked his crack addiction. He tricked for a while until one of his clients turned it into a serious relationship. He is now working full-time and planning on attending the University of New Orleans. At the end of his interview, Heath struck a hopeful note. "I got my shit together and I'm not trickin' anymore. And I found someone who actually gives a shit about me."

Our Personal Journeys

JEFF PALMQUIST:

I knew I was gay in junior high school. I came out to my mom almost in passing when I was in the eighth grade. One day after school I was sitting at the kitchen table crying. When my mom asked me what was wrong I said "Mom, I think I'm gay." And all she said was "I know." It wasn't a big deal at all. Growing up we were Methodists. We went to church and prayed before meals but we weren't fanatics.

In high school I was an athlete. I was on the basketball team and ran track and I was even quarterback for the football team. My friends and teammates knew and they were cool about it, which is kind of amazing considering that was over twenty years ago in a small town in South Dakota. After high school, I went to a small liberal arts college to study sports medicine/athletic training. I did that for a while then I took some time off to go to Hawaii where a friend of mine was living. I fell in love with Hawaii. After a few months, my friend, with whom I was staying, gently suggested I might want to get a job. I took the hint and became a go-go boy at the local gay bar where I had become something of a regular. I danced for about a month and it really wasn't my thing. I just wasn't into it. I told the manager I wanted to quit and he offered me a job bartending. I did that for a while until I got island fever. Then I went back home to finish school. After college, I spent two years with the Denver Broncos as an athletic trainer.

The first time I came to New Orleans was in 1994 for a National Athletic Trainers Conference. I liked New Orleans a lot and started visiting on a regular basis. In 1999 I actually spent the summer in New Orleans working at a daiquiri shop on Bourbon. After the summer I went home to teach and as soon as the school year was over, I loaded up a U-Haul and moved to New Orleans. In addition to all its well-known charms, what really struck me about New Orleans was the openness of the gay community. What struck me most was that the doors of the gay bars were open and the crowd would often spill out on the sidewalk. That was a bold concept for me. Everywhere else I had been—and I traveled a lot—the gay bars kept their doors closed. I eventually got hired on at Lafitte's and for a brief while also worked as a flight attendant for Jet Blue.

FRANK PEREZ:

I spent the better half of 1994 in Wichita,

Kansas, undergoing intensive Christian therapy to change my sexual orientation. Clearly the therapy didn't work; at least not in turning me straight. Ironically, it did, however, help me come to terms with my gayness and accept myself for who I am. The program I was involved with was affiliated with *Exodus*, an international umbrella network of ex-gay ministries predicated on the belief that a person could, through prayer and faith in Christ, change his or her sexual orientation. The concept is fundamentally flawed at its core but at the time I desperately wanted it to be true.

I had grown up Catholic and although my parents were fairly progressive, I was still ashamed of my burgeoning desires when they surfaced in junior high school. I'm pretty butch so it wasn't hard to play it straight. In college I joined a fraternity and began fooling around with one of the other brothers. (Now, thanks to Facebook, I've discovered that almost half the guys in the fraternity were closet cases!) College was when I really began to explore my sexuality and the gay scene, which, in Baton Rouge at the time, was somewhat limited. New Orleans, of course, was only an hour and a half away.

I drank a lot at LSU and started doing some pretty serious drugs, in part because I'm a hedonist, but also in part to escape the realization I was gay. When partying got the best of me and it became clear I was going to flunk out of college, I converted to Evangelical Christianity. My conversion was not so much a disguise as it was an effort to change. I transferred to another college and became very involved with a student ministry. Upon graduating, I joined the ministry. After being licensed by the denomination as a minister, I went to yet another campus and pioneered a student ministry there. That lasted a few years.

I left the ministry under something of a cloud. Although I remained abstinent while leading the ministry, the inevitable pull of the truth proved too strong. When I found myself drawn into a gay relationship, I resigned the ministry. That was a crossroads. The church officials recommended I participate in an ex-gay ministry. I was doubtful it would work but I resolved to give it a try. Deep down, I knew this would be my last attempt to change.

I went to Kansas with an open heart and honest intentions, hopeful that the program would work. The program consisted of a group of guys living in a large house with a leader/counselor. During the day we all had jobs and at night we would meet for a group meal followed by therapy and prayer sessions. After several months, I was disabused of the fantasy that I could change. I don't know precisely what caused the proverbial light switch to flip on, but one morning it just hit me: this is all complete and utter bullshit. I had never been around so many gay men before and the experience did serve as an introduction of sorts to gay culture. I left the program with an emerging sense of my identity as a gay man. It was in Kansas that I took that most difficult step in the coming out process: I came out to myself.

Part Six
Epilogue

Epilogue

A Good Mix

IN THE COURSE OF COMPILING THE INFORMATION FOR THIS BOOK, nearly everyone we interviewed voiced the same reason for becoming a regular at Café Lafitte: they felt comfortable because it's such a friendly place, which is somewhat amazing considering the demographic mix of people who frequent the bar. Unlike most gay bars, Café Lafitte does not cater to a particular type. This characteristic probably stems to the fact that Lafitte's was well established before gay bars began to cater to specific sub-groups. On any given day or night, you may find at Lafitte's a couple of bears chatting amiably with a pair of twinks who may be sitting next to bevy of lesbians who are entertaining a straight couple that haplessly wandered into the bar while a drag queen plays video poker not far away, and in the corner next to the eternal flame, an elderly gentleman tries to attract the attention of a twenty-one-year-old hustler who just sashayed in. Age, color, wealth, orientation, and scene preference are irrelevant at Lafitte's, checked at the door, if you will. Conversation flows easily, arrogance frowned upon. Clique-ish it is not.

Facilitating this friendly atmosphere are the bartenders, who are encouraged to know patrons by name and introduce them to each other as well as to visitors. For years there was a sign in the employee break room that read, "What are their names?" One bartender in the 1970s used to write guest's names in chalk on the bar until he remembered them. At many gay bars, bartenders tend to be aloof, if not outright snooty, toward any customer that isn't young or good-looking or doesn't dress "the right way." Not so at Lafitte's. Everyone is treated as a guest, the only exception being bums and addicts looking for a handout. Manager Paul Hammond formally adopted this attitude in 1997. Hammond, who was from a casino background, encouraged the bartenders to thinks of people as guests, not customers.

With such a business philosophy (and copious amounts of alcohol), it's easy to see why it's so easy to hook up with perfect strangers at Lafitte's. More than a few chance meetings have turned into long-term relationships.

Longtime regular Adam recalls meeting his lover one Tuesday afternoon in 1996. In those days the balcony was open seven days a week. After ordering a drink, Adam stepped onto the balcony to take in the afternoon air. And there was Jonathon. A friendly hello turned into a fourteen-year relationship that continues to thrive today.

Kevin Petefish, who has traveled the world and lived in several countries, comments on what makes New Orleans' gay bars unique:

> One of the first things that I noticed about New Orleans is that the gay bars weren't hidden away on some back street. The doors were wide open onto Bourbon Street. There were no back alley entrances, the boys were right out in the open even to the point of hanging outside on the sidewalk in plain view of gawking tourists.
>
> The bars in New Orleans were much smaller than the ones that I had been to in Texas. They are so big that there are lots of places to hide in. There is a forced intimacy in the bars in New Orleans due to their size. You really have to speak to someone when they are literally in your face. Also there really is no way of avoiding someone even if you want to.
>
> There is also the weather factor. People tend to dress very casually here due to the heat and humidity. I think that this has an equalizing effect on socializing. There is also more flesh on display due to less clothing. This adds to the sexual tension that already exists in gay bars.
>
> Crowds tend to show up later at the bars here due to them closing very late or not at all. You can always tell who the tourists are by how early they get drunk. I have noticed that there isn't the social stigma about being a "lush" as in other

places. There is no shame in getting drunk on a regular basis in New Orleans.

And although Café Lafitte is a gay bar, it does play host to a handful of straight couples. Here's how one such couple feels about the bar:

> When we started coming to the bar, we only knew one or two people, but enjoyed the music and the regulars of the place. Some of the folks there that are regulars did not take to us at the beginning, but instead tolerated us or preferred we rather not be there. I felt discriminated. After a while of hanging out over there, being introduced to the regulars and locals, that all changed. Now, we are like family there, get invited to many of the events and "TO DO's" and feel comfortable with our new friends that feel like very old friends when around them. Shawn (a bartender) typically jokes with me about "You ain't too bad for a White, straight guy." It is nice to know that there are people you can actually trust with your wallet in their hands and probably your life in their hands.

Another straight man, Timothy, remembers moving to New Orleans after his life in Texas had gone to pieces. He had one friend in the city, a gay man who frequented Café Lafitte. Thus, this was the first bar he went to in New Orleans. On his inaugural visit he was introduced to legendary bartender Aletha. Upon hearing his story, Aletha simply and sincerely said, "Welcome home." Tim remembers being "blown away." "I never felt so welcome anywhere. That was awesome."

It is said that Lisa Marie Presley, of all people, echoed this sentiment one afternoon as she and her son were walking down Bourbon Street. As they passed the bar, her son asked what the rainbow flags meant. Presley answered, "They mean everybody's welcome."

In Exile

The View from Behind the Bar

DAMON MARBUT IS A BARTENDER AT LAFITTE'S. His insights are representative of what it means to be gay in New Orleans. Damon in his own words:

When I came out at age twenty-one, in 2000, if anyone would have told me I'd one day be working in the most popular gay neighborhood bar in the French Quarter of New Orleans, and happily at that, I may have choked such a theory out of their assumptive throats. I was in business school, in transit between two Alabama universities, on track to attend law school and become, at some point and in highly ambitious theory, a corporate in-house lawyer for Merrill-Lynch or Viacom. I didn't have time for second guessing myself, let alone others doing it.

I stumbled into my job at Café Lafitte in Exile after a year of stopping off there, homeward bound, from managing a restaurant off Iberville across the Quarter. Being hired at the bar was an accident. The bartenders knew me as a pensive sort, reclusive almost, who kept to himself and his beers at two in the morning, rejecting advances from the drunk regulars and out-of-towners who would later become my closest friends. When I quit my job, I returned to Café Lafitte three nights in a row for what I didn't then recognize as solace and familiarity I'd grown to depend on. That had become my bar, as it had others twice my age. I felt a sense of ownership in it along with them. And when I was offered a fill-in position while another bartender was out of post-surgery commission for six weeks, I assumed it would be a smart way to have income until I found something better. I was given a full-time spot three weeks in and have never left. It is now my home, my bar, my livelihood (of course), as well as where I belong. I, like so many others, have inadvertently established an identity there, an identity that cannot be compared reasonably to any other I've had in the past.

The gay community in New Orleans is contradictory. Dichotomous, I should say. Paradoxical, yes. On one hand you have people pretending to be rigid, abrasive personalities just to mask the reality of their true kindness. On the other hand you have people pretending to be warm and generous who are subconsciously hiding their salacious and dysfunctional motives. To exist in this city is relatively easy, but to live here, I think this particular social tug-of-war must be given at least some credence. I've lived here for two years, and it took me almost the entirety of them to understand this, after so much trial and error. I spent a lot of time observing those who've lived here longer, those who have existed here longer, too, to get to the point I can discuss my perspective with a modicum of confidence. I, like most who persevered and earned the work-to-play lifestyle we all know too well, am an established man in this town I can't see myself ever leaving.

What has drawn me into a relationship with Café Lafitte is the history of the bar itself, as well as my co-workers who have been there for decades. I am thirty-two years old as I write out these thoughts, and have been in the service and hospitality industry since I was fifteen, but I am thankfully cognizant of the fact I don't have a toehold in universal bar life, or work life for that matter. And so, the "always a student, never a teacher" dictum remains with me. Lafitte's has a camaraderie amongst regular guests and locals and visitors from across the globe, and my suspicion is that this sense of welcome is borne of the endurance required in the distant past for us to have this luxury now. When I came out, I had a phenomenal friend network. My biggest concern was familial separation. The people who paved the road for the life I have now, we all have now, had far more concern for their safety before they even consciously considered their happiness. What I can only do is guess their happiness was a backburner issue behind survival. When I play catch-up with family and friends, and they ask where I work, these are the first things I think of before I even tell them the name of my bar. I am fortunate to be where I am, but I can't tell them this and expect them to understand. Expectations are dangerous, anyway. I just tell them I'm having a good time and it seems to satisfy them.

As an even younger man, I was curious about my country at large and traveled the United States, living in several states and visiting innumerable cities. From Oregon to Illinois to Georgia to Arkansas to Idaho and, of course, my home town of Mobile, Alabama, there is no gay scene in the country quite like ours in New Orleans. I experienced in my travels small, segregated clusters of communities beneath the canopy of one over-arching one, identified by a common sexual orientation. But the gay community in New Orleans is predominantly inclusive, which means an openness to all walks of life. When a heterosexual couple visits my bar and asks if it's okay that they're there even though they're straight, my common response has been, "As long as you're nice and having fun, no one here cares who you sleep with." So gender, ethnicity, tax bracket or age do not matter at Café Lafitte in Exile; the importance of our continuous enjoyment of the bar is built upon the collective

Epilogue

effort of staff and guests to feed the environment with warmth and good conversation. I think this immediate part of our history has been upheld well by all contributing members of our community. The friends I have made in my bar span generations and experiences, and as I have much more to learn as I evolve within what I consider my new hometown, I hope to be a component of positive presence at Café Lafitte that, if and when my time to move on comes, is one of fond recollection and memory.

A Mutual Affinity

IN THE COURSE OF MULTITUDES OF INTERVIEWS with dozens of gay men, one common thread emerges: the vast majority of them are not from New Orleans but consider her their "spiritual home" like Tennessee Williams put it, Joel Wilson, a former bartender at Lafitte's, echoes the sentiments of many:

> When I was growing up in Mississippi, New Orleans was an almost unspoken and constant part of my life. My family's farm was close enough to the city to make a day trip, but far enough away for this to be a rare occurrence. Before I had been able to start figuring out who I really was, and what's more, really wanted to be, random stories of New Orleans ran away with my imagination and my heart, spurring a deep-seeded love for the city I had never really known. In my head it became this place of wonder, a sort of long-lost sense of home. New Orleans was ever-present in my mind, and in my heart I knew one day that is where I would end up. I never thought I would live there forever, but I knew it would forever be my home.
>
> Upon moving to the city and witnessing the devastation that Katrina had wreaked upon her, I

felt what had been missing in my life since I was very young. There was a sense of relaxed determination that fought against every instinctual fiber of my brain, but slowly worked its way into my soul, and now when I visit my original home, I feel crazed and anxious to feel the broken sidewalks under my feet and to smell the dark smell of the night against the river.

New Orleans permeates her residents immediately, and sometimes before they arrive at their destination. She calls people to her, almost begging to know if they are strong enough to be her lover. The city is alive and she is a vicious lover, but if she deems you worthy to walk her lonely streets then her embrace is warm and more pleasurable than any ecstasy of human bonds.

This sense of connection to the city is virtually universal and transcends age differences and geographical origins. Many came to New Orleans to escape the doldrums of the small towns in which they grew up. Just as many others came never intending to stay but did. Falling in love with New Orleans is easy to do and it's certainly not a gay phenomenon; thousands of straight people as well have succumbed to New Orleans' well-chronicled seductions. Nonetheless, there is a certain affinity between gay men and New Orleans. This sense of belonging goes beyond the quaintness and charm of a lingering European atmosphere for which New Orleans is known. The connection is deeper, more psychic and rooted in a metaphorically shared experience. Historically, the gay experience in America is remarkably similar to the city's experience, namely one of difference, indifference, and difficulty.

Just as gay people in America have always been, and continue to be, considered "other," which is to say be defined by what they are not and devalued because of that difference, so too has New Orleans been considered "other." Both New Orleans and the gay person challenge and complicate the easy

Epilogue

black-and-white dualistic mentality that permeates so much of Western thought.

Within a few years after its meager founding as a French colony, Louisiana (which then meant primarily New Orleans) was essentially abandoned by the French crown and eventually handed over to Spain because it had become an unwanted burden. The colony proved to be just as much of an unprofitable nuisance to Spain, and after a meager forty years, Spain gladly disowned the colony and gave it back to France, who, in a matter of weeks, eagerly sold it to the United States. Both France and Spain considered New Orleans a colonial failure, which is to say, not what they expected, nor what they hoped for. The city resisted Americanization and the ensuing Creole-American conflict remains legendary. Except for the golden decades before the Civil War when New Orleans was a mighty economic power, New Orleans has consistently been a disappointment to its parent nation. Yet throughout that disappointment—perhaps because of it, perhaps in spite of it—New Orleans has managed to forge its own way and carve out an identity for itself that remains truly unique. Marinating for almost 300 years now, New Orleans has endured great adversity: constant floods and hurricanes, fires, diseases, governmental neglect, political corruption, wars, etc. and in the process has created a genuine culture that is wholly its own.

Some astronomers no longer refer to the universe; instead they speak of the Multiverse. The idea is that our universe is just one among many parallel universes. These sky wizards predict that eventually, billions upon billions upon trillions of years from now, after all the stars die, after all the planets and moons fall out of their orbits, after the remaining black holes fade away, all that will remain from all that is will be the fragmented and decayed remnants of time in the form of tiny photon particles traveling chaotically, spasmodically in a quantum realm—silent echoes of existence, in memoriam.

The existence of *our* familiarity, that is, for there is so much more than we have dreamt of in our philosophies. One of the most exciting theories in cosmology today is M Theory, which posits that each universe is merely a bubble floating in an infinite cosmological membrane. And when these bubbles collide there is, in one magical moment, a big bang, just like the one that gave birth to our little bubble 13.7 billion years ago—creation by collision, if you will, and so wonderfully random. What's more fascinating is that each universe-bubble may have its own set of physical laws, laws which may be entirely foreign and antithetical to the ones Sir Isaac Newton made so clear for us all.

New Orleans is a universe unto itself—a parallel existence born of a collision of cultures that continues to morph and expand and create and delight and surprise. It's a place where the established rules don't apply and contradictions are the norm rather than the exception. Consider the following phenomenon: once a year, on All Saints Day, the natives picnic in the city's many graveyards at the tombs of their dead relatives. The Ursuline Convent, the oldest Catholic Convent in the U.S., is just a few blocks away from the nation's oldest gay bar. Piety Street is just one block over from Desire Street. The sun rises on the west bank of the Mississippi River. Funerals are celebrated with jazz parades and the dead are buried above ground. Drive-through liquor stores and daiquiri shops are ubiquitous and it's legal to buy a fifth of whisky at a gas station at 4:00 a.m. on a Sunday. The rich and the poor share neighborhoods and shop at the same corner groceries and drink at the same corner bars. Perfect strangers greet each other with affectionate phrases like "Hey babe," or "Where yat dawlin." And each spring, the city's elite conservative businessmen don satin tights and very fey masks and prance around the streets throwing beads to, and partying with, the plebian masses.

In New Orleans, you learn to expect the unexpected. Contrary juxtapositions—sociological, moral, political, economic, religious, sexual—are manifold; they abound everywhere. Trying to make sense of them is for those who don't "get" it. Apollo and Dionysus peacefully coexist here. To ask why or how is to ask the wrong question. In New Orleans, binary oppositions not only converge, they mutate into an ever-changing rhizomatic wonderland, the only proper response to which is a shrug of the shoulders and a smile.

Unlike the majority of straight people who "get it" but are still initially puzzled by the contradictions that make New Orleans, gay men understand such contradictions instinctively and completely. The city's culture of carnal indulgence, its constant threat of destruction, its fervent judgment by the morally self-righteous, its status as *different*—these are all characteristics with which gay men can immediately identify. For what else does it mean to be a young man in our heterosexual society coming to grips with his homosexuality than to worship the flesh, to fear for his emotional and physical life, to suffer the slings and arrows of rejection and alienation, to be agonizingly aware that he is not like other boys?

But beyond all this, there is something else that under girds the bond between gay people and New Orleans: her unconditional acceptance and the open arms with which she receives and embraces people. New Orleans is a Siren City that smiles on all who visit her. She takes you in her arms and willfully gives up her secrets as she whispers in your ear, "It's okay. I'm not perfect either. Look at my scars and wounds and wrinkles. Let's forget the past with all its pain and live in the now. Come dream with me."

It is precisely this warm invitation that has inspired writers and artists for centuries. Many of them have commented on this notion of City as muse. Take for instance William Faulkner, who, once in a letter to his mother, described how accepted he felt in New Orleans, accepted in a way he had not experienced in other places.

This phenomenon baffles many people. Such people often remark how distinctive New Orleans is, how unlike any other American city it is. Not just the food and music but something deeper. What they sense but can't quite put their finger on is the fact that New Orleans has always resisted "cookie-cutter-ness."

After the Industrial Revolution effectively ended Jefferson's vision of America as an agrarian utopia, New Orleans could have evolved into the Queen City of the South (for a brief while she was) but to do so would have meant buying into the economic gospel of the capitalist barons who have succeeded in transforming America into a corporate feudalistic state. But old-fashioned, stubborn New Orleans resisted the sales pitch and ceded that honor to Atlanta and Houston, preferring instead to grow slowly, more authentically. New Orleans is many things but cutting-edge is not one of them.

Even today the familiar landmarks of corporate landscapes and urban fiefdoms that make every town look just like every other town are noticeably absent in New Orleans. Indigenous restaurants outnumber fast food and chain restaurants by astronomical numbers. Ditto for hotel chains. Not a single Fortune 500 Company is based here. Giant supermarkets have tried for years to make inroads here, mostly to no avail. And when Wal-Mart announced plans to open a "Super Center," the local population went ballistic, successfully delaying the store's opening for years. Shopping malls in the traditional sense are nowhere to be found in the city limits.

Like those who are proudly out, New Orleans is a city that knows herself well and is secure and confident enough in herself to extend an open hand and a warm smile to any and all, but at the same time it is fiercely protective of its culture and heritage, and that doesn't include fealty to corporate overlords. Like the flamboyant drag-queen who fiercely resolves to be herself regardless of what others think, so it is with New Orleans. Given the live-and-let-live attitude that defines New Orleans, it is no wonder gay men are drawn to the city.

Also cementing the strong bond between gay men and New Orleans is a common insight into the nature of reality and fantasy. At her core, New Orleans is a fascinating study in desire—its pull, its promises, its lies, and its consequences. Just as desire permeates the notion of gayness, defines it, really, for good or ill, so is desire inextricably linked with the heart of New Orleans. This fixation with desire is what fuels Carnival and Mardi Gras, the music and culinary scenes, the city's epic obesity and its rampant alcoholism.

Tennessee Williams came as close as anyone to explaining this phenomenon. It's no mistake he set his most famous play

Epilogue

on Elysian Fields. Elysian Fields Avenue was where Stanley and Stella lived in *A Streetcar Named Desire*. Upon arriving in New Orleans, Blanche Dubois says, "They told me to catch a streetcar named Desire and then transfer to one called Cemeteries." Anyone wanting to discover the secret to understanding and appreciating New Orleans should begin by considering the metaphorical implications of that quote. The easy conclusion is that desire leads to death, but The Big Easy is not that easy. No, the truth of the matter is that the folks here are keenly aware of their own mortality and it's that grim awareness that feeds the urgency of desire. Who knows what dreams may come in that sleep of death, so we better live it up while we have the time. Many of the men we interviewed for this book, especially the ones who moved here as adults, returned over and over again to the time they were lost in the closet, fumbling around in the dark, some spending years living double lives or going through the motions of being married for appearance's sake.

Elysium is a good way to describe New Orleans for both are mythical places that defy easy description or definition. For Homer and Pindar, Elysium was the final resting place for the souls of the heroic and the virtuous, a designation that would be complicated by later writers. Dante's Limbo in *The Divine Comedy* strongly resembles classical Elysium with one important difference—as the upper circle of hell, sadness prevails for the virtuous pagans who find themselves there; heaven is close yet unattainable. Renaissance poets envisioned the place as a paradise filled with joyful indulgences. In the fiction of Tolkien, Elysium is a mythical land of gods and elves and other fantastical creatures.

In all these literary depictions, Elysium is positioned on the margins of the afterworld, located off center, on the edge. And so it is with New Orleans: on the edge of the continent, on the edge of imagination, on the edge between life and death. To be gay in America is certainly to identify with such marginalization.

For Tennessee Williams, New Orleans *is* Elysium. For the gay man as well as for New Orleans, objective reality is adapted to the ideal, not the other way around. In other words, reality is adapted to the way things ought to be. Here the boundary between fantasy and reality is both malleable and permeable.

Blanche Dubois comes to New Orleans to escape the reality of her past and to begin her gradual decent into madness. But that's ironic because although New Orleans is a city filled with people living in what appears to be a fantasy world, their Blanche Dubois-ian denial of reality is not so much an escape as it is an alternative reality—an Elysium where broken dreams are welcomed and redeemed and given new life. The ghosts of past failures and previous loss are present for sure, but they are harmless; their power to haunt usurped by a new reality. At one point in the play, Blanche sings, "It's Only a Paper Moon," whose lyrics declare if both lovers believe their imagined reality, then it's no longer make believe. New Orleans and her many lovers couldn't agree more.

Much of New Orleans lies below sea level and is ever sinking, yet the people here, gay and straight, live with their heads in the clouds—hovering aloofly between heaven and earth, blithely ignoring that murky boundary between reality and fantasy, the line between life and death obscured by desire, all the while solemnly aware of their own impending mortality.

The Granddaddy of Them All

THIS GRIM AWARENESS is what makes New Orleans a city of traditions. Whether it be the euphoria of Mardi Gras or the devastation of Katrina, the life affirming music of a jazz funeral or the grief of burying a loved one, the exhilaration of the Saints singular Super Bowl victory or the agony of forty years of losing, the immense comfort of a sloppy roast beef debris po' boy or the rampant poverty of a sluggish economy, New Orleans is a city that feels and feels deeply. Voltaire observed the world is a tragedy to those that feel and a comedy to those that think. And when tragedy is a constant visitor, traditions abound. Traditions provide stability amid turmoil and security in the face of uncertainty.

Gay New Orleans has experienced not only the ups and

Epilogue

downs of the city itself but also manic episodes unique to the gay community. Gay New Orleans is not without its traditions and Café Lafitte in Exile is its oldest and most enduring. Billed as "The Granddaddy of them all," the bar has achieved a beloved and revered status among its descendents. The grandfather metaphor works well: Café Lafitte is old, wise, and constant. And, like grandfathers who have grandchildren who may not think them "cool," Café Lafitte knows that assessment will change with maturity. And when trendy-ness becomes not so important and the bars that are so "in" now fade away, it's a safe bet that Café Lafitte will be waiting with a warm heart and a big smile.

Appendices

Appendices

Appendix A
Gay Bars Throughout New Orleans History

ATTEMPTING TO COMPILE an exhaustive list of all the gay bars that have existed in New Orleans throughout its history is a daunting task. The following list of gay bars and their locations was assembled primarily from the recollections of the people we interviewed. You will see that several bars changed names several times over the years. These changes are denoted with an arrow →.

Listings without a street name indicate conflicting memories of where the bar was located or incomplete property records.

Late nineteenth c.- Brothel for male prostitutes run by Miss Big Nelly

1933 - Café Lafitte in Exile (Bourbon)
1939 - Dixie's Bar of Music in CBD, later on Bourbon where Cat's Meow now is

1940s/50s - Club My-O-My Sho-Bar on Lakefront

1950s
Wanda's (Iberville)
Mom's Society Page (Exchange Alley)
Tony Bacino's (where the Dungeon is now) (Toulouse)
The Society Page → Le Round-Up (1967) (St. Louis)

1960s
The Golden Lantern (Royal)
Mabel's Cove (N. Rampart)
Upstairs Lounge - arson in 1973 (Chartres & Iberville)
Midship - Managed by Miss Fury (Iberville)
The Chart House - was nicknamed "The Wrinkle Room" because it catered to older men (Chartres)
Gregory's → Wild Side → The Doubleplay (Dauphine & St. Louis)

Charlie's Corner (Decatur & Gov. Nichols)
Chelsea's (Bourbon)
Decatur House (Decatur)
Entre Nous (Decatur)
Fat Sam's (N. Rampart)
The Galley House (Chartres & Toulouse)
Jewel's Tavern (Decatur)
Le Jardin (Conti & Dauphine)
Linda's (Esplanade)
Lucille's (St. Philip)
Poco Loco (Chartres)
Diogynes
Trocadero (Burgundy)
Tush (N. Rampart)
Enraged Chick (St. Mary)

1971 - Travis', A Sho-Bar, → Wolfendales → Starlight by the Park → Michael's on the Park (N. Rampart)

1970s

Flamingo's (St. Charles)
Gigi's (N. Rampart)
Safari House
Quarter Horse
Vicki's (Decatur)
Cruz Inn → Millie's → The Post Office → The Corner Pocket (1983) (Burgundy & St. Louis)
Pino's → The Other Side (Elysian Fields)
Charlene's → The Mint → The Matrix → Moulon Rouge → It's About Time → John Paul's
Brady's → Diane's → Mona's → Lindsey's → Applause → North Star— We Are Family → Sundance → Footloose → The Ninth Circle (N. Rampart & St. Peter)
The Fatted Calf (St. Peter)
The Country Club (Louisa)
Smokin' Mary's → The Phoenix (1983) (Elysian Fields)
The Caverns→ The Bourbon Pub (1976) (Bourbon & St. Ann)

1980s

The Friendly Bar (Chartres in the Marigny)
2601 - where Mimi's now is (Marigny)
Menefees → The Monster (N. Rampart)
Finale 2 → Town Hall → The Bar at Congo Square (N. Rampart)
Grog → Partners → Bends → Iggy's (1987)
Soiled Dove Saloon
Elaine's
The Louisiana Purchase → The Warehouse → Good Friends (1986) (Dauphine & St. Ann)
Tigers→ Play it Again, Sam → Rawhide (Burgundy & St. Ann)
Ruby Fruit Jungle (Frenchmen then Decatur)
The Refuge (corner of Royal & Ursiline)
MRB used to be a gay bar (St. Phillip)
Paw Paw's → The Sterling → CD's Saloon → Burgundy House → The Front Page → 700 Club (Burgundy & St. Peter)
Leo's → Pete's (1982) → LeBistro → Oz (Bourbon)
The Cabaret (N. Rampart)
Hits
Big Daddy's (Royal)
Loading Zone (Bourbon)

1990s & 2000s

The Copper Top → The Blue Moon Saloon → Chet's → Cutters
Travis 2 → TTs West → 7th Circle (N. Rampart)
Cow Pokes→All Ways Lounge (St. Claude)
Napoleon's Itch (Bourbon)

Appendix B
Historical Timeline of Gay Mardi Gras

1949 - Fat Monday Luncheon debuts at Brennan's Restaurant/New Orleans.

1958 - Krewe of Yuga/New Orleans, first gay Carnival club debuts.

1962 - Krewe of Petronius/New Orleans debuts. Yuga/New Orleans ball raided.

1963 - Bourbon Street Awards debuts at Bourbon at Dumaine Streets.

1966 - Krewe of Amon-Ra/New Orleans debuts.
Krewe of Armeinius/New Orleans debuts.

1969 - Amon-Ra/New Orleans presents first Miss America Pageant.

1970 - Mystick Krewe of Apollo/New Orleans debuts at Monteleone, first gay ball presented in a hotel.

1971 - Krewe of Olympus/New Orleans debuts, first gay ball presented at St. Bernard Civic Auditorium.

1972 - Mystick Krewe of Apollo/New Orleans, first gay ball to debut at Municipal Auditorium.

1977 - Mystic Krewe of Celestial Knights/New Orleans debuts.
Academy of the Golden Goddess, Inc. (AGGI)/New Orleans debuts presenting annual awards show celebrating gay Carnival clubs.

1979 - Police strike cancels parades/New Orleans; Charlene's and The Golden Lantern group takes to the street as the Krewe of Cancellation.

1980 - Police cancel Krewe of Cancellation parade/New Orleans, no parade permit.

1981 - Krewe of Ishtar/New Orleans, first all-lesbian club debuts.

1982-3 Ed Smith hosts Bourbon & St. Ann St. Awards/New Orleans, no Bourbon Street Awards held.

1983 - The Krewe of Polyphemus/New Orleans debuts.

Appendices

1984 - Lords of Leather/New Orleans, first leather Carnival club debuts.
Eleven gay Carnival krewes present balls, a record/New Orleans
No Edd Smith or Bourbon Street Awards/New Orleans.

1986 - Bourbon Street Awards/New Orleans returns and moves to St. Ann & Burgundy.

1987 - Krewe of Queenateenas/New Orleans debuts presenting first Official Gay Mardi Gras Bead Toss, 828 Bourbon St.

1991 - AGGIs/New Orleans end.

1992 - Petronius, Amon-Ra, Armeinius, and Lords of Leather present only gay balls/New Orleans.

1993 - Krewe of Barkus/New Orleans parade hits the streets of the French Quarter.

1994 - Krewe of Queenateenas/New Orleans crown first King Cake Queen of Gay Mardi Gras.

1999 - First new gay Carnival Club since 1984, Krewe of Mwindo/New Orleans debuts.

2000 - le Vendredi de Nuit Mardi Gras Avant/New Orleans debuts benefiting AIDS service organizations.

2001 - People of Substance's Krewe of Anubis/New Orleans debuts.

2002 - Bourbon Street Awards/New Orleans returns to Bourbon & St. Ann Streets.

2003 - Krewe of Satyricon/New Orleans debuts.

Appendix C
Southern Decadence Grand Marshals

SDGM I Frederick Wright, 1974
SDGM II Jerome Williams, 1975 (deceased)
SDGM III Preston Hemmings, 1976
SDGM IV Robert Laurent, 1977
SDGM V Robert King (deceased) and SDGM VI Kathleen Kavanaugh, 1978
SDGM VII Bruce Harris, 1979
SDGM VIII Tom Tippin, 1980
SDGM IX Tommy Stephan, 1981
SDGM X Don Ezell, 1982 (deceased)
SDGM XI Danny Wilson, 1983 (deceased)
SDGM XII Mumbo, 1984
SDGM XIII Michael "Fish" Hickerson, 1985
SDGM XIV Kathleen Conlon, 1986
SDGM XV Olive, 1987
SDGM XVI Jerome Lebo, 1988 (deceased)
SDGM XVII George Goode, 1989 (deceased)
SDGM XVIII Ruby, 1990 (deceased)
SDGM XIX Jamie Temple, 1991
SDGM XX Rhee, 1992 (deceased)
SDGM XXI Ms. Fly, 1993 (deceased)
SDGM XXII Alain, 1994 (deceased)
SDGM XXIII Blanche, 1995
SDGM XXIV Wayne White, 1996
SDGM XXV Miss Love, 1997
SDGM XXVI Robin Malta, 1998 (deceased)
SDGM XXVII Errol Rizzuto, 1999
SDGMs XXVIII Tony Langlinais and Thom "Smurf" Murphy (deceased), 2000
SDGMs XXIX Bianca Del Rio, Pat "Estelle" Ritter, and Rick Thomas, 2001
SDGM XXX "Irish" Mike Sheehan, 2002
SDGM XXXI Rusty LaRoux, 2003

Appendices

SDGM XXXII Donald "Donnie 'Jager' Jay" James, 2004 (deceased)

SDGM XXXIII Lisa Beaumann and Regina Adams, 2005

SDGM XXXIV Lisa Beaumann and Regina Adams, 2006

SDGMs XXXV: Tittie Toulouse and Paloma, 2008

SDGMs XXXVI: Tittie Toulouse and Paloma, 2009

SDGMs XXXVII: Julien Artressia and Toby Lefort, 2010

SDGMs XXXVIII: Tiffany Alexander and Misael Rubio, 2011

Appendix D
Victims of The Upstairs Lounge Fire - June 24, 1973

Louis Horace Broussard, 26
Joe William Bailey, age unknown
Leon Richard Maples, age unknown
Clarence McCloskey, Jr., age unknown
James Curtis Warren, age unknown
Robert Keith Lumpkin, 29
Eddie Hosea Warren, age unknown
John Thomas Golding, Sr., age unknown
Willie Inez Warren, 47
Perry Lane Waters, Jr., age unknown
Douglas Maxwell Williams, Jr., age unknown
Donald Walter Dunbar, age unknown
Kenneth P. Harrington, 48
William R. Larson, age unknown
Adam Roland Fontenot, age unknown
David Stuart Gary, age unknown
Glenn Richard Green, age unknown
Horace W. Getchell, Jr., age unknown
Joseph Henry Adams, Jr., 26
James Walls Hambrick, 45
Guy D. Anderson, age unknown
Gerald Gordon, age unknown
Duane George Mitchell, age unknown
George Steven Matyi, age unknown
Ferris Leblanc, age unknown
Luther Boggs, 47
Larry Stratton, 25
Herbert Dean Cooley, 32
Unknown
Unknown
Unknown
Unknown

Appendix E
Early Gay Activists in New Orleans

Larry Bagneris, Jr., political activist
Roberts Batson - co-founder of LAGPAC in 1980; president of
the Bienville Foundation
Karen Button - Celebration co-chair, 1984-1986
Betty Caldwell - co-founder of PFLAG New Orleans
Chris Daigle - LAGPAC, 1990s
Pat Denton - member of the first LAGPAC Board in 1980
Karl Eskovich - early and long-time NO/AIDS advisor on
disability benefits
Mae Falgout - LAGPAC, 1980s
Mark Gonzales - attorney and activist
Billy Henry - early co-chair of Gay Pride and tri-chair of 1993
National PFLAG Conference
Dr. Michael Kaiser - AIDS activist from the very beginning of
the epidemic
Dr. Niki Kearby - co-founder of PFLAG New Orleans
Joan Ladiner - Lesbian activist in the 1980s and 1990s
Clay Latimer - Lesbian activist
Crystal Little - Transgender activist from the 1980s to present
Rich Magill - journalist for gay community in the 1980s and
The Upstairs Lounge fire writer
Joe Melcher - chair of the PFLAG/NO Scholarship Committee
Loretta Mims - Lesbian activist in the 1980s
Melanie Miranda - member of the first LAGPAC Board in 1980
Rip and Marsh Naquin-Delain - first domestic partners
registered with the city, journalists
John Ognibene - president, Crescent City Coalition, 1980s
Alan Robinson - co-chair, LAGPAC, 1980s; Co-founder, The
Gertrude Stein Society
Bill Rushton - co-founder, The Gertrude Stein Society
Rich Sacher - political activist in the 1980s
Courtney Sharp - Transgender activist and long-time PFLAG
Board member

In Exile

Jack Sullivan - attorney and political activist
Mike Stark - founder, Gay Services Center
Julie Thompson - chair, PFLAG New Orleans
Johnny Townsend - chronicler of Upstairs Lounge Fire
Linda Tucker - life partner of Charlene Schneider
Noel Twilbeck - HIV/AIDS activist
Jerry Zachary - founder of New Orleans Gay Men's Chorus in
     1980

Appendix F
Prominent Gay New Orleanians

Enrique Alferez, sculptor
Larry Bagneris, Jr., civil rights leader, political activist
Bryan Batt, actor
Poppy Z. Brite, writer
Truman Capote, writer
Ellen DeGeneres, comedienne, TV personality
George Dureau, artist
Skylar Fein, artist
Tony Jackson, musician
Francis B. Johnston, photographer
Rex Reed, film critic, cultural essayist
Christopher Rice, writer
Lyle Saxon, writer, preservationist
Clay Shaw, businessman, preservationist
John Kennedy Toole, writer
Tennessee Williams, playwright
Walt Whitman, poet

Appendix G
Partial Transcript of a 2007 meeting of the New Orleans Human Relations Commission, with Commentary[94]

IN 2001, AN OPENLY GAY MAN, Larry Bagneris, was appointed as executive director of the New Orleans Human Relations Commission, an arm of the mayor's office. Bagneris has a long history of advocating for equality and civil rights. He was the first openly gay person elected as a delegate to the National Democratic Convention in NYC in 1980 and in 2002 was elected to the board of directors of the International Conference for Gay and Lesbian Elected Officials.

In 2007, Bagneris convened a "listening session" of the Human Relations Commission focused on the gay, lesbian, and transsexual community in New Orleans. Wood Enterprises General Manager Ken GranPré served as co-chair. A transcript of the meeting reveals key insights into the state of the post-Katrina gay community in New Orleans. The first speaker at the meeting was local gay historian Roberts Batson, who was asked to survey local gay history:

> Thank you. I'm supposed to give you the lesbian, gay, bisexual, transgender history of New Orleans. I can give it to you within about ten seconds. Things used to be bad, they're a lot better now.

Batson goes on to describe the historical invisibility of gay life:

> One of the preconceptions that has borne on and angers me, if you try to research our history it's

---

94 The full transcript is on file with the New Orleans Human Relations Commission -City Hall
1300 Perdido Street, Room 8E07 New Orleans, LA 70112

very difficult to do. I say that because up until the modern era, almost every, whatever you want to call it, same identifying people, same sex identified people, were doing everything possible to keep from being identified as such. Because you were burned at stake, you were arrested, you were thrown in prison; you were shot. It's so frustrating that we have a whole part of our history so forever hidden from us. So you just have to try to kind of read between the lines. If you go to the old microfilm at The Times-Picayune, you go through it and say, "Where is the written record of our existence?" We know that we have been here. About the only thing that you will find written are stories about arrests. And that is pretty much my documented history, and that enrages me because what that does not show is, it does not show the rest of our lives. It doesn't show all of the wonderful creativity as far as our outrageousness and flair, and yes, being fabulous in everything possible. It also doesn't tell the stories of courage, tremendous acts of courage. When I read about them I am always deeply, deeply moved. And it also doesn't tell the stories of friends and lovers taking care of each other.

Randy Evans from the Forum for Equality on legal strides made by the gay community in recent years:

As a community, our first real accomplishment was in 1990 and that was with the passage of the Human Rights Ordinance. Prior to that time the community had attempted on two other occasions to pass an ordinance in New Orleans and had been unsuccessful. Basically at that time there were essentially two elected officials who wouldn't even give the gay and lesbian community the time of day. Most elected officials would not even meet with our community, were not interested in addressing any of our concerns. So we basically went out politics in forums, the way that politicians do. And we got involved in a big way, donating money, putting in volunteer hours, organizing voters, registering voters. We were able to pass the Human Rights Ordinance, which basically affects housing, public accommodations, and employment for gays and lesbians in New Orleans. That was a huge accomplishment. Then in 1993 we actually got passed the Domestic Partnership Ordinance; that was a really scaled back version of domestic partnership. If you read about things that are being passed now, it really is the equivalent of marriage or maybe marriage-like, this was pretty much a registration proceeding with very limited benefits. It was more designed to allow the individuals to go to their own employers and participate in company benefits that might be offered if somebody was registered as a partner. And that really is the place that our community needs to move next in New Orleans.

Derrin Bergeron of the Human Rights Campaign on other political victories:

HRC more focuses on federal legislation, but especially where it's important in states to where it can change the views in that state to focus back here. In other words, like Mary Landrieu, she has been very supportive. She co-sponsored the hate crimes legislation and ENDA;[95] she has cosponsored all of that. So when she is up for

---

[95] Employment Non-Discrimination Act

reelection, HRC has posted for her that she is their number one target to get her reelected. It is that important because she is a vote for us. So that is where we focus on in all that, all right? So, thank you. Like I said, it's important. Sometimes we live here in New Orleans and—well then the other really important thing I think that we don't have to really worry about because of the change that was made in Congress in 2006, which is Marriage Equality. You have your first domestic partnership registrants' right here [indicating] Rip and Marsha Naquin-Delain. [Audience applause.] It's important that we all want to say, you know, "Let us love who we want to love." And that is what HRC is focused on doing. Thank you.

Executive Director Bagneris on divisions within the community:

I grew up in a community where women and men didn't even communicate until AIDS came along and lesbian sisters came out to take care of us. I grew up in a community where we fought over not allowing transsexual people to turn this movement into just that issue and yet they were all a part of the community, included bisexuals. Where do we get this from? I mean, we have a great community, particularly in the City of New Orleans; that has caused to learn to live together, blacks, whites, browns and yellows, you see it every weekend, you see it during the week. We've got women, men working together in groups and in everything else. I mean; I really want to know.

Chairperson Ken GranPré on the diversity and tolerance of New Orleans:

You know, I want to say something. I've only been

here for 15 years. I lived in San Francisco for three and a half years and after that I lived in Toronto. I lived in Key West, I lived in Chicago. I have lived all over the country. And what you're talking about, Larry, this city and I comment this to tourists all of the time. This is the most openly gay city that I've ever lived in. In San Francisco you don't drive by and see the doors to the gay bars wide open with people standing out on the sidewalks, you don't see that. You don't see people in San Francisco outside the cat strolls holding hands with same sex people, you don't see that. And I think living here for 15 years and after seeing what I have seen in all of these cities, it's because New Orleans, gay, straight, black, white, is the most accepting city of other people. New Orleans is the city of diversity and I think that is one thing that we have all been very proud of. I think that is one thing that we have all worked really hard at. I don't know if you agree with that or not, but that is my observation of New Orleans after living here for 15 years.

Local citizen Bryan Sims on gay pride:

I have lived here for 18 years. It is interesting when you are talking about the community here, because I just got back from PRIDE weekend in Boston and Toronto. And I think that it's interesting because here we didn't have a parade this year and you can look at that a couple of different ways. But where in these cities the parades went on for so long it got to the point where we were like, "How much prouder can you get?" You know, between Southern Decadence, Halloween, Mardi Gras and now the Gay Easter parade, we don't necessarily need to have a parade just to be proud and I think that is positive thing. And at the same time I have never been prouder of the city, talking about inclusiveness than when a few years at the St. Patrick's Day Parade in New York and Boston were not allowing gay people to enter, and here, Pete's was one of the places welcomed in. That sense of and in terms of what I would like to bring to the table here today, in rebuilding the city and it talks to what you brought up what you [indicating] talked about, the people who are coming in here. I don't know if that, if this is necessarily within the purview of this commission, but I think that in some ways whether it be the mayor's office or the Convention and Visitors' Bureau, need to do some outreach to get people coming here to this city. And of course it extends to every community, but given the topic here tonight, why can't someone, some entity from New Orleans work toward promoting or providing information to those? You know, such events as the PRIDE festivals throughout the country, saying that we have respect in this community here, Patrick's tours, information, whatever, that is not my expertise. Whenever I meet people at these events and tell them to come on down, they say, "Oh, yeah, we'd love to, but..." They don't know; many people in Canada, they don't know what Southern Decadence is. You have to explain it to them. Many people all around the rest of the country don't. And if we don't start getting more people of every type into this city on a regular basis, it's a worry. Because I'm telling you, I am coming from working on Royal Street and let me tell you, it's quiet over there these days. Anyone else here in the service industry knows that, and if that doesn't change, we may not continue to have a community left to fight about. At the same time we need to get more people involved who would be able to participate. I see a lot of people in this room whom I have known for years who are actively involved, which is great. I don't see a lot of say 20 something's out here. And that is interesting, because up in Toronto that is what the crowd is. People have become so accepting and inclusive that the gay people, guys and gals, just go out to any bar. So I think that is something that we need, to have a critical mass and get more people, to get a new generation to fight the fight.

Community Center worker Mary Griggs on the lack of communication among various segments of the gay community:

One of the things that I really think we need to do is have more communication. I mean; I found out about this meeting because Tim sent an email out from the Forum.[96] I had no idea about this meeting and I know that a lot of people that would've been here if the word had gotten out. There are plenty of ways to communicate, whether it be a Yahoo group or posting on other places, and I think that is what we needed to do as part of the community. We all have our own separate groups. We have listing groups, religious groups, community centers, et cetera. There has to be more communication between us and between the government to us so that we can refer them among our membership. I was, you know, able to rearrange my schedule to come to this meeting, but I only found out about it on Thursday. So that is why there aren't that many people here. I belong to about nine or ten different groups that I could have spread the

---

[96] The Forum for Equality

information too, had I known about it earlier in advance. And I think that is to the detriment of our community, you know. Yes, it's lovely that we are diverse. We have a great diversity, we have a great tolerance of all different kinds, but we are not communicating to one another or, you know, to others. That is what I wish for, you know, we've got to communicate and you all need to communicate to us too.

MR. GRANDPRE': Well in defense of that, the Ambush donated two half-page ads for the last month announcing this meeting. So it was advertised.

MS. GRIGGS: Yeah, now I certainly see that, but as a lesbian I don't do much of the bar reading. I do get it and I read one or two sections of it. So yes, I do have the Ambush but I don't read it page to page because it doesn't necessarily speak to, you know, the things that I'm doing outside of the bar or areas that are applicable.

MR. SIMS: Can I just follow up with that? I understand your point, but how you get the message out is one step, but it's also people caring enough to come here. I think that is one of New Orleans' double-edged sword. I know we have a great community, but it's getting people involved. Among the community, we have a limited number of individuals. Unlike areas such as New York or Boston, I would think that this area would be packed. Of course here it's like "let the good times roll." I mean; how do you create that community involvement?

Pastor Darren Harris of the Freedom Fellowship Community for Greater New Orleans on the divide between the white and black gay communities:

> I was listening to a lot of the conversation and of
> course I know Roberts and some others. And I see
> Dexter within the community, but one of the
> things that I realize is that, and it's a wonderful
> thing for us to be diverse and to have this
> diversity and talk about inclusion. It's wonderful
> to include all of the different communities, even
> with the LGTB community as well. But I noticed
> even in this room and a couple of the other
> meetings that I have been in, there is, I think even
> though it's not intentional, there is still some
> communities that are excluded even though we
> are trying include communities. I wanted to say
> that there is an African American part of the
> LGTB community who are not represented and
> who are not here. And of course it could be due to
> communication, like Mary stated. It could be due
> to the fact that they don't feel that they are part of
> this LGTB community.

Rabbi Ed Cohn of Temple Sinai agreeing with Pastor Harris:

> RABBI ED COHN: Well, I am trying to raise
> consciousness to the fact that one of the
> wonderful things about the LGTB and one of the
> bigger challenges of LGTB herein New Orleans is
> that we are still segregated and striated just as the
> whole greater community.

Author's Note: On the issue of racial division within the
gay community in New Orleans, the majority of our white
interview subjects never brought the subject up, but virtually
all of the African American subjects did. James Broussard, for
example, a graduate of Xavier University who now lives and
works in the French Quarter, regularly visits straight bars in

the black community that host "gay nights," notably Seals (which offers drag shows on Thursdays) and Fusion, on St. Bernard Avenue.

Appendix H
Photographs

Café Lafitte in Exile as it appeared in the 1960s and as it appears today. Prior to 1953, the bar was located at 941 Bourbon, present site of Lafitte's Blacksmith Shop. (Photo from the archives of Wood Enterprises and Jeffrey Palmquist)

Enrique Alferez was a prominent artist whose sculpture adorns the Lakefront Airport, City Park, the Charity Hospital building and other landmarks throughout New Orleans. Alferez was a regular at Café Lafitte in Exile and designed the distinctive shape of the bar as well as the bar's trademark flame fountain. (Photo by Dan Leyer. The Historic New Orleans

Collection, accession number 1981.324.2.403. Gift of Allan Phillip Jaffe.)

Lyle Saxon was a writer, visionary and preservationist who tirelessly promoted the French Quarter as a cultural and artistic haven. He was the first of a number of literati to frequent Café Lafitte in Exile. (Photo courtesy of The Historic New Orleans Collection, accession number 1983.215.75. Gift of Ms. Gretchen Crager Sharpless).

Marsha and Rip Naquin-Delain was the first couple in New Orleans to register as domestic partners. They founded and continue to publish *Ambush*, the Gulf South's oldest gay magazine. Photo courtesy of Rip and Marsh Naquin-Delain.

The corner of Iberville and Chartres Streets and the site of **The Upstairs Lounge** fire. Photo courtesy of Jeffrey Palmquist.

An invitation to the first **Southern Decadence**. It reads:
"Ya'll come to the Dress Up As Your Favorite Southern
Decadent Party at Belle Reve, 2110 Barracks, late afternoon,
Sunday September 3rd."
Image courtesy of SouthernDecadence.com.

Long-time Lafitte's bartender **Aletha** performs at the
annual Red Party, 2008.
Photo courtesy of Jeffrey Palmquist.

Appendices

A Note on Interview Subjects

INTERVIEWS WERE CONDUCTED in person when possible but when not feasible were done via phone and/or e-mail. Some people requested we not use their real names for a variety reasons and we have respected their wishes. They are not included in the following list of interview subjects. We are grateful to everyone who agreed to be interviewed. In addition to the people we formally interviewed, we gleaned information from dozens of others in casual conversations at various bars throughout New Orleans.

Sebastian Alexander, Will Antill, Brandon Barrois, Bennett, Willamena, Charlie Bezou, Matthew Boudreaux, James Broussard, Stewart Butler, Aletha Bryant, Jerry Buillott, Albert Carey, Ryan Carrere, John Castille, Santa Claus, Victor Cody, Tracey Cox, Rachel Dangermond, Gilbert Estrada, Randy Evans, Skylar Fein, Otis Fennell, Bill Fitch, Will Fowler, Dr. Jody Gates, John Gotthelf, Ken GranPre, Jan Hauser, Wayne Hendon, Brett James, Andrew Jones, Eric Hess, Dr. Niki Kearby, Dr. Calvin Kilcrease, Andrew Kingswell, Tim Kinzel, Myke Kolb, Ray Lassere, Clay Latimer, Toby Lefort, Crystal Little, Damon Marbut, Marcy Marcell, Cha Cha Martinez, Paul Melancon, Bartley Mulligan, Dr. John Meyers, Marsha Naquin-Delain, Rip Naquin-Delain, Jon Newlin, Philip Palumbo, Max Peinado, Kevin Petefish, Billy Phillips, Tim Power, Shawn Rossi, Cary Rowbatham, Javier Sandoval, Lloyd Sensat, David Seruntine, Jack Sullivan, John Tinsley, Corey Torres, Victory, Chris Ward, Joel Wilson, Tim Wolff, David Woodall.

Bibliography

Quotes

Dayries, Provosty A. Quoted in Scott Ellis' *Madame Vieux Carré: The French Quarter in the Twentieth Century.* Jackson, MS: UP Mississippi, 2010. Print.

Isherwood, Christopher. Quoted in Charles Kaiser's *The Gay Metropolis.* Houghton Mifflin. 1997. Print.

Weinstein, Jeff. Quoted in *The Celluloid Closet.* Vito Russo. New York: Harper & Row, 1981. Print.

Introduction

Batson, Roberts. "New Orleans." *glbtq.com.* glbtq, inc., 2004. Web. <http://www.glbtq.com/social-sciences/new_orleans.html>

Dawdy, Shannon Lee. *Building the Devil's Empire French Colonial New Orleans.* Chicago: U Chicago P, 2008.

Faulkner, William. "The Tourist." *The Double Dealer* 1925.

Part One: Pre-1960: The Closet Door Creaks

Adams, Nordette. "New Orleans Walt Whitman and *Leaves of Grass.*" *Examiner.com.* Examiner.com. Web. April 11, 2009.

Batson, Roberts. "New Orleans." *glbtq.com.* glbtq, inc., 2004. Web. <http://www.glbtq.com/social-sciences/new_orleans.html>

Bossu, Jean Bernard. *Travels in the Interior of North America, 1751- 1762.* Trans. Seymour Feiler. Norman: U Oklahoma P, 1962.

Bibliography & Index

Brennan, Ella. "The Secret Ingredient." *My New Orleans*. Ed. Rosemary James. New York: Touchstone, 2006.

Brothers, Thomas. *Louis Armstrong's New Orleans*. New York: W.W. Norton, 2006.

Brown-Saracino, Japonica. "Social Preservationists and the Quest for Authenticity." *City & Community* 3.2 (2004): 135-56. Print.

Bryant, Linda Goode, dir. *Flag Wars*. Zeitgeist Films, 2003. Film.

Byrne, Peter. "Two Cheers for Gentrification." *Howard Law Journal* 46 (2003).

Capote, Truman. *Other Voices, Other Rooms*. Random House: New York, 1948.

Codrescu, Andrei. *New Orleans, Mon Amor*. Chapel Hill: Algonquin Books, 2006.

Ellis, Scott S. *Madame Vieux Carré: The French Quarter in the Twentieth Century*. Jackson, MS: UP Mississippi, 2010.

Fair, Lucy J. "New Orleans." *Encyclopedia of Homosexuality*. New York: Garland Publishing, 1990. Print.

Faulkner, William. "The Tourist." *New Orleans Sketches*. Ed. Carvel Collins. Jackson, MS: University Press of Mississippi, 2002.

Fellows, Will. "The Gay Penchant for Preservation." *National Trust for Historic Preservation*. Web. n.p., n.d. <http://www.preservationnation.org/issues/diversity/lgbt-heritage-in-preservation/penchant-for-preservation.html>

---. *A Passion to Preserve*. U Wisconsin P. 2004.

Folsom, Ed. and Kenneth M. Price. Eds. *The Walt Whitman Archive*. Web. <http://www.whitmanarchive.org/>

Friedman, Nancy. *Art of the State: Louisiana*. New York: Harry N. Abrams, Inc., 1998.

Glatzer, Richard and Wash Westmoreland, dirs. *Quinceanera*. Cinetic Media, Kitchen Sink Entertainment LLC, 2006. Film.

Griffin, Farah Jasmine. *Who Set You Flowin'? The African-*

American Migration Narrative. New York: Oxford UP, 1995

Kaiser, Charles. *The Gay Metropolis.* New York: Houghton Mifflin, 1997.

Kinney, Robert. *The Bachelor in New Orleans.* New Orleans: Bob Riley Studios, 1942. Cited in Ellis, Scott S. *Madame Vieux Carré The French Quarter in the Twentieth Century.* Jackson: UP Mississippi, 2010.

Knopp, Jr., Lawrence M. "Gentrification and Gay Community Development in a New Orleans Neighborhood." Diss. U of Iowa, 1989. Print.

---. "Some Theoretical Implications of Gay Involvement in an Urban Land Market." *Political Geography Quarterly* 9.4 (1990): 337-52. Print.

Liebling, A.J. *The Earl of Louisiana.* Baton Rouge: LSU Press, 1970.

Martin, Robert K. "Whitman, Walt." *glbtq.com.* New England Publishing Associates, 1995, 2002. Web. <http://www.glbtq.com/literature/whitman_w.html>

Saxon, Lyle. *The Friends of Joe Gilmore.* New York: Hastings House, 1948.

Thomas, James W. *Lyle Saxon: A Critical Biography.* Birmingham, AL: Summa Publications, 1991.

Toole, John Kennedy. *A Confederacy of Dunces.* New York: Grove Press, 1980.

Vidal, Gore. *The City and the Pillar.* New York: E.P. Dutton & Co., 1948.

Von Reizenstein, Ludwig. *The Mysteries of New Orleans (Die Geheimnisse von New Orleans)* Trans. Steven Rowan. John Hopskins UP. 2004.

Whitman, Walt. "I Saw in Louisiana a Live Oak Growing." *The Norton Anthology of Modern Poetry.* Eds. Richard Ellmann and Robert O'Clair. New York: W.W. Norton & Co., 1988.

Zukin, Sharon. "Gentrification: Culture and Capital in the Urban Core." *Annual Review of Sociology* 1987.

Part Two: The 1960s: The Closet Door Inches Open

Boyer, Lori. "The Caillot Manuscript." *Mardi Gras Guide* 2011: 48-49.

Brite, Poppy Z. *Prime: A Novel.* New York: Three Rivers Press, 2005.

Butler, Judith. *Gender Trouble: Feminism and the Subversion of Identity.* New York, Routledge, 1990.

Cary, Albert J. "New Orleans Mardi Gras Krewes." *glbtq.com.* glbtq, inc., 2004. Web.
< http://www.glbtq.com/social-sciences/new_orleans_mgk.html>

Clendinen, Dudley, and Adam Nagourney. *Out for Good.* New York: Simon & Schuster, 1999.

Durant, Will and Ariel. *The Story of Civilization: The Age of Louis the XIV.* New York: Simon & Schuster, 1963.

Kirkwood, James. *American Grotesque.* New York: Harper, 1992.

Lambert, Patricia. *False Witness: The Real Story of Jim Garrison's Investigation and Oliver Stone's film JFK.* New York: M. Evans and Co., 1998.

Paglia, Camille. *Sexual Personae: Art and Decadence from Nefertiti to Emily Dickinson.* New York: Vintage, 1991.

Smith, Howard. "Golden Celebration." *Mardi Gras Guide.* 2011.

Starr, S. Frederick. *New Orleans Unmasqued.* New Orleans: Dedeaux Publishing, 1985.

White, Edmund. *States of Desire Travels in Gay America.* New York: E.P. Dutton, 1980.

Wolff, Tim. "The Sons of Tennessee Williams." WYES-TV, New Orleans. February 18, 2011. Television.

Part Three: The 1970s: Some Damn Fool Kicks the Closet Door Wide Open

Fein, Skylar. *Remember the Upstairs Lounge.* 2010.

Maginnis, John. *The Last Hayride*. Baton Rouge: Gris Gris Press, 1984.

Rechy, John. *City of Night*. New York: Grove Press, 1963.

---. "City." http://www.johnrechy.com/city.htm

Sears, James T. *Rebels, Rubyfruit, and Rhinestones Queering Space in the Stonewall South*. New Brunswick, NJ: Rutgers UP, 2001.

Summers, Claude J. *glbtq.com*. "George Dureau." glbtq, inc., 2002. Web. <http://www.glbtq.com/arts/dureau_g.html>

White, Edmund. *States of Desire Travels in Gay America*. New York: E.P. Dutton, 1980.

Williams, Tennessee. *Memoirs*. New York: New Directions Books, 1972.

Part Four: The 1980s: The Closet Door Falls off Its Hinges

Badgett, M.V. Lee. *Money, Myth, and Change The Economic Lives of Lesbians and Gay Men*. Chicago: U of Chicago P, 2001.

Chasin, Alexandra. *Selling Out: The Gay and Lesbian Movement Goes to Market*. New York: Palgrave, 2000.

Gluckman, Amy and Betsy Reed, eds. *Homo Economics: Capitalism, Community, and Lesbian and Gay Life*. New York: Routledge, 1997.

Witeck, Robert and Wesley Combs. *Business Inside Out Capturing Millions of Brand Loyal Gay Consumers*. Chicago: Kaplan, 2006.

Part Five: The 1990s & 2000s: Yellow Brick Roads Emerge from the Closet

Batson, Roberts. "New Orleans." *glbtq.com*. glbtq, inc., 2004. Web. <http://www.glbtq.com/social-sciences/new orleans.html>

Bienvenue II, Robert V. "The Development of Sadomasochism as a Cultural Style in the Twentieth-Century United States." Diss. Indiana University, 1998.
Feiler. Norman: U of Oklahoma, 1962.

Brando, Marlon, perf. *The Wild One*. Columbia Pictures. 1953. Film.

Lewis, Pierce F. *New Orleans The Making of an Urban Landscape*. Charlottesville, VA: U Virginia P, 2009.

Magill, Rich. *Exposing Hatred A Report on the Victimization of Lesbian and Gay People in* New Orleans, LA. Louisiana Lesbian and Gay Political Action Caucus, 1991.

Maginnis, John. *The Last Hayride*. Baton Rouge: Gris Gris Press, 1984.

Rice, Christopher. "Death and Rebirth." *The Advocate*. 11 Oct. 2005: 47.

Thompson, Mark, ed. *Leatherfolk: Radical Sex, People, Politics, and Practice*. New York: Alyson, 1992.

Yeats, William Butler. "The Second Coming." *The Norton Anthology of Modern Poetry*. Eds. Richard Ellmann and Robert O'Clair. New York: W.W. Norton & Co., 1988.

Index

Bilbliography & Index

About the Authors

Jeffrey Palmquist grew up in South Dakota and now lives in the French Quarter, where he is a bartender at The Café: Lafitte in Exile.

Frank Perez grew up in Louisiana and now lives in the French Quarter, where he is a barfly at The Café: Lafitte in Exile.

About the Publisher

"...taking the reader down a different path."

Established in 2008, **LL-Publications** is based in Scotland, UK and produces fiction and nonfiction both in paperback and in multiple ebook formats. Our talented authors represent both sides of the Atlantic.

We are proud to be a small, independent press providing **quality** over **quantity**. Our motto is "taking the reader down a different path" because the titles we publish are not recycled, formulaic plots with predictable characters in uninspired settings. We publish books that readers will remember.

We do not follow trends.

With that in mind, we invite you to take a short Reader Experience Survey to get your feedback on this book and your reading experience. Please go to the following web page:

www.ll-publications.com/33243.html

Your opinion is truly appreciated!

Best wishes,

LL-Publications
www.ll-publications.com

Other Titles by LL-Publications

Oil and Water...and Other Things That Don't Mix
Anthology to raise funds to aid the Gulf Coast clean-up
Edited by Zetta Brown and Nicky Wheeler-Nicholson Brown
ISBN: 978-1-905091-85-0 (print)

The BP oil spill disaster in April 2010 prompted authors Zetta Brown and Nicky Wheeler-Nicholson Brown from the *She Writes™* online community of writers to develop the charity anthology *Oil and Water...and Other Things That Don't Mix.* All proceeds will be divided between The Bay Area Food Bank (www.bayareafoodbank.org) and MOBILE Baykeeper® (www.mobilebaykeeper.org) to aid their continuing mission to help the Gulf Coast communities affected.

The anthology features award-winning authors, poets, journalists, bloggists, newly published authors, and talented new authors making their debut writing on the official theme "Conflict...Resolution optional." The stories, poems and recollections will make you laugh, cry, think—and some may even get you angry.

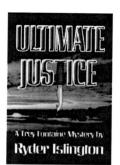

ULTIMATE JUSTICE
A Trey Fontaine Mystery
Ryder Islington
ISBN 978-1-905091-78-2 (print) / 978-1-905091-79-9 (ebook)

Special Agent Trey Fontaine has his hands full as he tries to juggle three different sets of cases in his hometown of Raven Bayou, Louisiana. While healing from a bullet wound, and on limited duty, he is charged with helping find out what's happening to young women who are disappearing without a trace. But that's just the beginning. Someone is beating and raping women in town, women who are related to his godfather, Detective Russell Coleman. And then the bodies of men start showing up, eviscerated. Are the crimes related? Or are has the town become a haven for all sorts of criminals? Can Trey stop the violence? Or will he only figure out the truth after someone he loves is dead?

The Hollows: Book One – The Ticking
By Ben Larken
ISBN: 9781905091546 (print) / 9781905091553 (ebook)
2011 EPIC eBook Award – Best Horror

1949: A young girl is traumatized when she witnesses a grisly murder in the forest behind her home.

1999: A loving wife disappears in the middle of the night, leaving no trace of her whereabouts.

2009: Former detective David Alders rents an apartment at a typical complex; a quiet unassuming place nestled in the outskirts of Fort Worth called The Hollows. Instead he finds terror, time travel, and murder—all for one low monthly rent.

Welcome to THE HOLLOWS.

Pray that the lease agreement expires before you do.

OOPS!
By Darrell Bain
ISBN: 978-1-905091-72-0 (print) / 978-1-905091-73-7 (ebook)

Oops! is the third collection of stories from multi-award winning author Darrell Bain written in the individual style that has kept Bain's readers coming back for more for the past twenty years.

When Cupid and a Gremlin bump heads, the sparks fly in a rare fantasy story by the author. Others stories in the collection include *A Simple Idea,* an almost ludicrously simple method of eliminating corruption and idiocy from the political process, one that has been around for centuries but gone unrecognized. *Cure for an Ailing Alien* finds a nurse who must come up with a cure for an alien, one whose bodily processes are completely unknown. You'll be amazed at her cure! *Retribution* is the story of unexpected consequences when alien meets human. *Robyn's Rock* is partially based on a happening in the author's life during a walk with his granddaughter.

Texas author Darrell Bain is a retired Vietnam vet and former Christmas tree farmer and the highly-successful author of over fifty books.
www.darrellbain.com

DEVIL DON'T WANT HER
By Zetta Brown
ISBN: 978-1-905091 -40-9 (ebook)

A humorous short story where a young, spiritually righteous woman, Faith Darling, must face the fact that you cannot escape from your family and the truth.

When Faith's notorious great-grandmother Miss Sunny Vincent dies, Faith, as the only surviving relative, must arrange the funeral. However, Miss Sunny Vincent's remains are hard to dispose of because God won't have her...and the Devil don't want her.

CPSIA information can be obtained at www.ICGtesting.com
Printed in the USA
BVOW08s1711111213

338816BV00003B/437/P

9 781905 091997